The Ultimate Mediterranean Diet Cookbook for Beginners

999+ Days of Flavorful, Easy Recipes with a 30-Day Meal Plan to Transform Your Health and Simplify Your Lifestyle, and Beautiful Full-Color Illustrations

Joy Carline

Disclaimer

The recipes and nutritional information in this cookbook are for informational purposes only. They are not intended as medical advice or as a substitute for the advice of your healthcare provider. Please consult your doctor or a qualified health professional regarding any specific dietary concerns or medical conditions before adopting any new nutritional regimen, including the Mediterranean Diet.

While the author and publisher have made every effort to ensure the accuracy and completeness of the information contained in this cookbook, they assume no responsibility for any errors or omissions. The author and publisher disclaim any liability arising from using or misusing the information presented herein.

Individual dietary needs vary, and all readers are encouraged to tailor the recipes to suit their preferences, dietary needs, and health goals. The nutritional information provided is estimated based on standard data and should only be used as a guide.

Table of Contents

Basics of the Mediterranean Diet

The Mediterranean Diet is more than a diet—it's a way of life that embraces the Mediterranean region's flavors, traditions, and health benefits. Rooted in the culinary practices of countries like Greece, Italy, and Spain, this eating style prioritizes whole foods, balance, and the joy of shared meals. It's no wonder the Mediterranean Diet is considered one of the world's healthiest and most sustainable diets.

What is the Mediterranean Diet?

The Mediterranean Diet is inspired by the traditional eating habits of Mediterranean cultures, particularly in the mid-20th century when heart disease rates in these regions were remarkably low. Unlike restrictive diets, it's a flexible, delicious approach to eating that emphasizes variety, fresh ingredients, and mindful consumption.

Core Components of the Mediterranean Diet

The Mediterranean Diet is built around natural, nutrient-dense foods, focusing on balance and flavor:
1. **Fruits and Vegetables**: These form the backbone of Mediterranean meals, offering a rainbow of nutrients, fiber, and antioxidants.
2. **Whole Grains**: Staple foods like whole-grain bread, brown rice, and bulgur provide energy and fiber.
3. **Healthy Fats**: Olive oil is the cornerstone of Mediterranean cooking, and it is accompanied by nuts, seeds, and avocados.
4. **Lean Proteins**: Fish and seafood are the primary proteins, with moderate amounts of poultry, eggs, and legumes. Red meat is limited.
5. **Diary**: Small portions of cheese and yogurt add flavor and calcium.
6. **Herbs and Spices**: Natural seasonings like oregano, thyme, and garlic enhance dishes without excess salt.
7. **Wine in Moderation**: Red wine is often enjoyed in small amounts, though optional.

Health Benefits of the Mediterranean Diet

1. Heart Health

The Mediterranean Diet is rich in heart-healthy fats, such as monounsaturated fats from olive oil and omega-3s from fish. These nutrients help reduce bad cholesterol and support cardiovascular health.

2. Weight Management

The diet promotes weight control through nutrient-dense foods that are naturally filling and satisfying. Unlike calorie-focused plans, it emphasizes quality over quantity.

3. Longevity and Disease Prevention

Research shows that people who follow the Mediterranean Diet tend to live longer and have lower risks of chronic diseases such as diabetes, Alzheimer's, and certain cancers.

4. Improved Mental Health

The Mediterranean Diet's emphasis on whole, unprocessed foods and omega-3-rich fish supports brain health, reducing symptoms of depression and cognitive decline.

5. Holistic Well-being

By focusing on mindful eating and shared meals, the Mediterranean Diet fosters emotional and social well-being, essential for overall health.

How to Incorporate the Mediterranean Diet into Your Daily Life

Adopting the Mediterranean Diet doesn't have to be complicated. Here's how you can easily make the switch:

Simple Swaps

- Replace butter with olive oil for cooking and dressing salads.
- Swap refined white rice for whole grains like quinoa or barley.
- Opt for fresh fruit instead of sugary desserts.

- Replace processed snacks with nuts, seeds, or roasted chickpeas.

Meal Planning Tips
- **Start with a Base**: Build meals around vegetables, whole grains, and legumes.
- **Add Protein**: Incorporate fish, seafood, or plant-based proteins like lentils and chickpeas.
- **Include Healthy Fats**: Use olive oil, avocados, or nuts to enhance flavor and satiety.
- **Prep Ahead**: Cook grains, roast vegetables, and prepare dips like hummus in advance for easy meal assembly.

Shopping for Ingredients
- Stick to the outer aisles of the grocery store where fresh produce, lean proteins, and dairy are located.
- Stock up on pantry staples like olive oil, canned tomatoes, whole grains, and dried herbs.
- Choose seasonal fruits and vegetables for maximum flavor and nutrition.

Cooking Techniques
- **Grill or Roast**: Highlight the natural flavors of vegetables, fish, and lean meats.
- **Sauté with Olive Oil**: Create flavorful bases for dishes with garlic, onions, and herbs.
- **Make It Fresh**: Use raw ingredients for salads, dips, and spreads like tzatziki or guacamole.
- **Simmer Slowly**: Develop deep flavors in soups, stews, and tomato-based sauces.

The Mediterranean Lifestyle: More Than Just Food

The Mediterranean Diet is about embracing a balanced lifestyle:
- **Be Active**: Physical activity is a natural part of Mediterranean living, whether walking, gardening, or dancing.
- **Share Meals**: Mealtimes are opportunities to connect with loved ones, fostering community and emotional well-being.
- **Savor the Moment**: Eating mindfully and enjoying each bite can enhance satisfaction and prevent overeating.

Embrace the Mediterranean Spirit

The Mediterranean Diet is about changing not just what you eat but how you live. By embracing fresh, wholesome foods and celebrating the joy of mealtime, you can improve your health, nurture your relationships, and enrich your daily life.

So, why wait? Start incorporating the principles of the Mediterranean Diet into your routine today. Your body, mind, and spirit will thank you for it.

Your free gift!

Scan the QR code to download the free
30-Day Meal Plan to Transform Your Health and Simplify Your Lifestyle.
We promise you'll love it!

Chapter 1. Breakfast Recipes

1. Greek Yogurt with Honey, Walnuts, and Fresh Berries

Yield: 2 servings | **Preparation Time:** 10 minutes | **Cooking Time:** None

Ingredients	Nutritional Information (Per Serving)
Base Ingredients • 1 cup plain Greek yogurt (full-fat or low-fat, as preferred) • 1 tbsp honey (adjust to taste) • 1/4 cup raw walnuts, roughly chopped • 1/2 cup fresh mixed berries (e.g., blueberries, raspberries, and sliced strawberries) **Optional Customizations** • 1/4 tsp ground cinnamon for a hint of spice • 1 tsp chia seeds for extra fiber and omega-3s • 1 tsp fresh mint leaves, finely chopped, for a refreshing touch	• **Calories:** 200 kcal • **Protein:** 10 g • **Carbohydrates:** 14 g • **Fats:** 10 g • **Fiber:** 2 g • **Cholesterol:** 5 mg • **Sodium:** 40 mg • **Potassium:** 220 mg

Equipment Needed
- Mixing bowl
- Two small serving bowls or glasses
- Measuring spoons

Step-by-Step Instructions

Step 1: Prepare the Ingredients
1. Wash the berries thoroughly and pat them dry using a clean kitchen towel.
2. Roughly chop the walnuts if not pre-chopped.

Step 2: Sweeten the Yogurt
1. Mix the Greek yogurt with 1/2 tablespoon of honey in a mixing bowl. Stir until the honey is evenly mixed. Taste and adjust sweetness by adding more honey if desired.

Step 3: Assemble the Bowls
1. Divide the sweetened yogurt evenly between two serving bowls or glasses.
2. Top each serving with an equal number of fresh berries.
3. Sprinkle the chopped walnuts over the berries for a crunchy texture.

Step 4: Add Optional Enhancements
1. If desired, sprinkle a pinch of ground cinnamon over each bowl for warmth.
2. Scatter chia seeds over the top for an extra nutritional boost.
3. Garnish with freshly chopped mint leaves for freshness and vibrant color.

Step 5: Drizzle with Honey
1. Finish each bowl with a light drizzle of the remaining honey to add a sweet, glossy finish.

Serving Suggestions
- **Breakfast:** Serve alongside a slice of whole-grain bread or a boiled egg for a complete meal.
- **Snack:** Enjoy as a stand-alone, energizing snack.
- **Dessert:** Layer the ingredients in a tall glass for an elegant parfait presentation.

---

2. Mediterranean Veggie Omelette with Feta

Yield: 2 servings | **Preparation Time:** 10 minutes | **Cooking Time:** 10 minutes

Ingredients	Nutritional Information (Per Serving)
Base Ingredients	- **Calories:** 210 kcal
• 4 large eggs	- **Protein:** 12 g
• 2 tbsp milk (optional, for fluffiness)	- **Carbohydrates:** 6 g
• 1/4 tsp sea salt (or to taste)	- **Fats:** 16 g
• 1/8 tsp ground black pepper	- **Fiber:** 1 g
• 1 tbsp olive oil	- **Cholesterol:** 220 mg
• 1/4 cup red bell pepper, diced	- **Sodium:** 400 mg
• 1/4 cup zucchini, diced	- **Potassium:** 250 mg
• 1/4 cup cherry tomatoes, halved	
• 1/4 cup red onion, finely chopped	
• 2 tbsp fresh parsley, chopped	
• 1/4 cup crumbled feta cheese	
Optional Customizations	
• 1/4 tsp smoked paprika or chili flakes for a spicy kick	
• A handful of spinach or kale for extra greens	
• Fresh basil or oregano for additional Mediterranean flavor	

Equipment Needed
- Medium mixing bowl
- Non-stick skillet (10-inch recommended)
- Spatula
- Cutting board and knife

Step-by-Step Instructions
Step 1: Prepare the Ingredients
1. Wash and dice the red bell pepper, zucchini, and red onion. Halve the cherry tomatoes.
2. Crack the eggs into a medium mixing bowl; add milk (if using), salt, and pepper. Whisk until the mixture is smooth and slightly frothy.

Step 2: Cook the Vegetables
1. Heat olive oil in the skillet over medium heat.
2. Add the red onion and bell pepper, cooking for 2–3 minutes until softened.
3. Stir in the zucchini and cherry tomatoes, cooking for another 2 minutes until the vegetables are slightly tender but still vibrant.

Step 3: Pour the Egg Mixture
1. Reduce the heat to low and evenly distribute the cooked vegetables in the skillet.
2. Pour the egg mixture over the vegetables, tilting the pan slightly to spread the eggs evenly.

Step 4: Add the Feta and Herbs
1. Sprinkle the crumbled feta cheese and half the fresh parsley evenly over the omelet.
2. Cover the skillet with a lid and cook for 3–5 minutes until the eggs are set and the cheese has slightly melted.

Step 5: Serve the Omelette
1. Use a spatula to gently fold the omelette in half or slide it whole onto a serving plate.
2. Garnish with the remaining parsley and any additional herbs or toppings you like.

Serving Suggestions

- Pair with a slice of whole-grain bread and a side of fresh greens drizzled with olive oil and lemon juice.
- Serve alongside fresh fruit or a simple tomato and cucumber salad.
- Enjoy herbal tea or a small glass of freshly squeezed orange juice.

This **Mediterranean Veggie Omelette with Feta** is a flavorful and nutrient-packed dish that reflects the richness of Mediterranean cuisine. With its emphasis on fresh vegetables, heart-healthy olive oil, and protein-rich eggs, it's a delicious way to enjoy the health benefits of this time-honored diet. Bon appétit!

3. Savory Olive Oil and Herb Muffins

Yield: 12 muffins | **Preparation Time:** 15 minutes | **Cooking Time:** 20 minutes

Ingredients	Nutritional Information (Per Muffin)
Base Ingredients	• **Calories:** 180 kcal
• 2 cups whole wheat flour	• **Protein:** 5 g
• 1 tsp baking powder	• **Carbohydrates:** 14 g
• 1/2 tsp baking soda	• **Fats:** 12 g
• 1/2 tsp sea salt	• **Fiber:** 2 g
• 1/4 tsp ground black pepper	• **Cholesterol:** 40 mg
• 2 large eggs	• **Sodium:** 200 mg
• 1/2 cup extra virgin olive oil	• **Potassium:** 110 mg
• 3/4 cup plain Greek yogurt	
• 1/4 cup milk (or plant-based alternative)	
• 1/2 cup crumbled feta cheese	
• 1/4 cup chopped fresh parsley	
• 1 tbsp chopped fresh thyme	
• 1 tbsp chopped fresh rosemary	
Optional Customizations	
• Add 1/4 cup sundried tomatoes, finely chopped, for extra flavor.	
• Substitute feta cheese with grated Parmesan or goat cheese.	
• Add 1/2 tsp smoked paprika for a subtle, smoky flavor.	

Equipment Needed

- Muffin tin (12 cups)
- Paper liners or non-stick spray
- Large mixing bowl
- Whisk and spatula

Step-by-Step Instructions

Step 1: Prepare the Oven and Muffin Tin

- Preheat your oven to 375°F (190°C).
- Line a muffin tin with paper liners or grease it with non-stick spray.

Step 2: Mix the Dry Ingredients

1. In a large mixing bowl, combine the whole wheat flour, baking powder, baking soda, sea salt, and ground black pepper.

Step 3: Whisk the Wet Ingredients

1. Whisk together the eggs, olive oil, Greek yogurt, and milk until smooth in a separate bowl.

Step 4: Combine and Fold

- Pour the wet ingredients into the bowl with the dry ingredients.
- Gently fold the mixture until just combined (do not overmix).
- Add the crumbled feta cheese, parsley, thyme, and rosemary. Fold until evenly distributed.

Step 5: Fill the Muffin Tin

1. Evenly distribute the batter among the 12 muffin cups, filling each about three-quarters full.

Step 6: Bake the Muffins

1. Place the muffin tin in the preheated oven and bake for 18–20 minutes, or until a toothpick inserted into the center of a muffin comes out clean.

Step 7: Cool and Serve

- Remove the muffins from the oven and let them cool in the tin for 5 minutes.
- Transfer them to a wire rack to cool completely or enjoy warm.

Serving Suggestions

- Serve warm with a dollop of tzatziki or labneh.
- Pair with a fresh green salad for a light Mediterranean meal.
- Enjoy as a savory snack with herbal tea or coffee.

These **Savory Olive Oil and Herb Muffins** are a delicious way to incorporate Mediterranean flavors into your diet. The olive oil and herbs provide heart-healthy fats and antioxidants, while the whole wheat flour and Greek yogurt offer fiber and protein for sustained energy. Enjoy!

4. Shakshuka with Spinach and Chickpeas

Yield: 2 servings | **Preparation Time:** 10 minutes | **Cooking Time:** 20 minutes

Ingredients	Nutritional Information (Per Serving)
Base Ingredients - 1 tbsp extra virgin olive oil - 1 small onion, finely chopped - 1/2 red bell pepper, diced - 2 cloves garlic, minced - 1/2 tsp ground cumin - 1/2 tsp smoked paprika - 1/4 tsp red chili flakes (optional, for heat) - 1 can (7 oz) diced tomatoes (or about 1 cup fresh tomatoes, diced) - 2 tbsp tomato paste - 1/2 can (7 oz) chickpeas, drained and rinsed - 2 cups fresh spinach, roughly chopped - 2 large eggs - 1/4 tsp sea salt (or to taste) - 1/8 tsp ground black pepper - 2 tbsp fresh parsley, chopped (for garnish) - 2 tbsp crumbled feta cheese (optional, for garnish) **Optional Customizations** - Add 1/4 tsp turmeric for extra depth of flavor. - Substitute kale for spinach for a slightly firmer texture. - Include 1 tbsp sliced olives for a briny Mediterranean touch.	- **Calories:** 230 kcal - **Protein:** 10 g - **Carbohydrates:** 18 g - **Fats:** 11 g - **Fiber:** 5 g - **Cholesterol:** 160 mg - **Sodium:** 380 mg - **Potassium:** 400 mg

Equipment Needed
- Medium-sized skillet with lid
- Wooden spoon or spatula

Step-by-Step Instructions

Step 1: Prepare the Base
1. Heat the olive oil in a medium skillet over medium heat.
2. Add the chopped onion and diced red bell pepper. Sauté for 5 minutes or until softened.
3. Stir in the garlic, ground cumin, smoked paprika, and chili flakes (if using). Cook for 1 minute, until fragrant.

Step 2: Create the Sauce
1. Add the diced tomatoes and tomato paste to the skillet. Stir to combine.
2. Reduce the heat to low and simmer for 5 minutes, allowing the flavors to meld.

Step 3: Add Spinach and Chickpeas
1. Stir in the chickpeas and spinach. Cook for 2–3 minutes, until the spinach is wilted.
2. Season with salt and black pepper to taste.

Step 4: Poach the Eggs
1. Make two small wells in the sauce with a spoon. Crack one egg into each well.
2. Cover the skillet with a lid and cook for 5–7 minutes until the egg whites are set and the yolks are cooked to your preference.

Step 5: Garnish and Serve
1. Remove the skillet from heat.
2. Sprinkle the shakshuka with fresh parsley and crumbled feta cheese (if using).

Serving Suggestions
- Serve with warm whole-grain pita bread or a slice of crusty sourdough for dipping.
- Pair with a simple side salad of cucumbers, tomatoes, and olives.
- Enjoy with a dollop of Greek yogurt for added creaminess.

5. Lemon and Ricotta Pancakes with a Honey Drizzle

Yield: 2 servings (approximately 6 pancakes) | **Preparation Time:** 10 minutes | **Cooking Time:** 15 minutes

Ingredients	Nutritional Information (Per Serving)
Base Ingredients • 1/2 cup whole wheat flour (or all-purpose flour for a lighter texture) • 1/2 tsp baking powder • 1/4 tsp baking soda • 1/4 tsp sea salt • 1 large egg • 1/2 cup ricotta cheese • 1/4 cup milk (or plant-based milk) • 1 tbsp fresh lemon juice • 1 tsp lemon zest • 1 tbsp extra virgin olive oil (or melted butter) • 1 tbsp honey (plus more for drizzling) **Optional Customizations** • Add 1/4 tsp vanilla extract for extra flavor. • Substitute honey with maple syrup for a different sweetness profile. • Top with fresh berries for added nutrients and color.	• **Calories:** 250 kcal • **Protein:** 10 g • **Carbohydrates:** 25 g • **Fats:** 11 g • **Fiber:** 2 g • **Cholesterol:** 90 mg • **Sodium:** 240 mg • **Potassium:** 150 mg

Equipment Needed
- Medium mixing bowl
- Whisk
- Non-stick skillet or griddle

- Spatula

Step-by-Step Instructions

Step 1: Prepare the Batter
1. whisk together the flour, baking powder, baking soda, and salt in a medium bowl.
2. combine the egg, ricotta cheese, milk, lemon juice, lemon zest, olive oil, and honey in another bowl. Whisk until smooth.
3. Gradually add the wet and dry ingredients, stirring until combined. Do not overmix; small lumps are okay.

Step 2: Heat the Skillet
1. Heat a non-stick skillet or griddle over medium heat. Lightly grease with olive oil or cooking spray.

Step 3: Cook the Pancakes
1. Pour 1/4 cup of batter onto the skillet for each pancake.
2. Cook for 2–3 minutes or until bubbles form on the surface and the edges look set.
3. Flip the pancakes and cook for another 1–2 minutes or until golden brown.
4. Transfer the pancakes to a plate and repeat with the remaining batter.

Step 4: Serve and Garnish
1. Stack the pancakes on a serving plate.
2. Drizzle with honey and, if desired, garnish with fresh berries, a dollop of ricotta, or a sprinkle of extra lemon zest.

Serving Suggestions
- Pair with a side of Greek yogurt and a fresh fruit salad.
- Enjoy a herbal tea or freshly squeezed orange juice for a refreshing Mediterranean breakfast.

This **Lemon and Ricotta Pancakes with a Honey Drizzle** recipe combines Mediterranean staples like olive oil, honey, and fresh citrus to create a light yet satisfying dish. Packed with protein, healthy fats, and natural sweetness, these pancakes are a delightful way to start your day with a taste of the Mediterranean Diet. Enjoy!

6. Whole Grain Toast with Avocado, Tomato, and Za'atar

Yield: 2 servings (4 slices) | **Preparation Time:** 10 minutes | **Cooking Time:** None

Ingredients	Nutritional Information (Per Serving)
Base Ingredients • 4 slices whole grain bread • 1 ripe avocado • 1/2 cup cherry tomatoes, halved • 1 tsp fresh lemon juice • 1/2 tsp sea salt (or to taste) • 1/4 tsp ground black pepper • 1 tsp za'atar seasoning • 1 tbsp extra virgin olive oil **Optional Customizations** • Add a sprinkle of red chili flakes for heat. • Top with crumbled feta cheese for added creaminess. • Garnish with fresh parsley or basil for extra freshness.	• **Calories:** 280 kcal • **Protein:** 6 g • **Carbohydrates:** 30 g • **Fats:** 16 g • **Fiber:** 8 g • **Cholesterol:** 0 mg • **Sodium:** 280 mg • **Potassium:** 480 mg

Equipment Needed
- Toaster or skillet (for toasting bread)
- Fork (for mashing avocado)
- Knife and cutting board

Step-by-Step Instructions
Step 1: Toast the Bread
1. Toast the whole grain bread slices in a toaster or dry skillet over medium heat until golden and crisp.

Step 2: Prepare the Avocado
1. Cut the avocado in half, remove the pit, and scoop the flesh into a small bowl.
2. Add the lemon juice, salt, and black pepper. Mash with a fork until smooth but slightly chunky.

Step 3: Assemble the Toast
1. Spread a generous layer of mashed avocado onto each slice of toasted bread.
2. Top with halved cherry tomatoes, arranging them evenly over the avocado.
3. Sprinkle a pinch of za'atar seasoning over each slice.

Step 4: Add the Finishing Touch
1. Drizzle extra virgin olive oil over each toast for a rich Mediterranean flavor.

Serving Suggestions
- Serve with mixed greens drizzled with olive oil and lemon juice.
- Pair with a boiled egg or Greek yogurt for a protein boost.
- Enjoy with a cup of herbal tea or freshly squeezed orange juice.

This **Whole Grain Toast with Avocado, Tomato, and Za'atar** is a delicious and healthful example of the Mediterranean Diet's emphasis on fresh, wholesome ingredients. Packed with heart-healthy fats, fiber, and vibrant flavors, it's a quick and satisfying meal option for any time of day. Enjoy!

7. Fresh Fruit Salad with Mint and Citrus Dressing

Yield: 2 servings | **Preparation Time:** 15 minutes | **Cooking Time:** None

Ingredients	Nutritional Information (Per Serving)
Base Ingredients • 1/2 cup fresh strawberries, hulled and sliced • 1/2 cup fresh blueberries • 1/2 cup diced melon (such as cantaloupe or honeydew) • 1/2 cup orange segments, peeled and chopped • 1/2 cup red or green grapes, halved • 1 tbsp fresh mint leaves, finely chopped **Citrus Dressing** • 2 tbsp freshly squeezed orange juice • 1 tbsp freshly squeezed lemon juice • 1 tsp honey (or maple syrup for a vegan option) • 1/2 tsp orange zest • 1 tsp extra virgin olive oil (optional, for richness) **Optional Customizations** • Add a sprinkle of cinnamon for a warm spice note. • Substitute the melon with pineapple for extra sweetness. • Include a handful of pomegranate seeds for a burst of color and flavor.	• **Calories:** 130 kcal • **Protein:** 2 g • **Carbohydrates:** 30 g • **Fats:** 1 g • **Fiber:** 4 g • **Cholesterol:** 0 mg • **Sodium:** 5 mg • **Potassium:** 250 mg

Equipment Needed
- Large mixing bowl
- Small whisk or fork (for the dressing)

19

- Zester or fine grater
- Knife and cutting board

Step-by-Step Instructions

Step 1: Prepare the Fruits
1. Wash all the fruits thoroughly under running water.
2. Hull and slice the strawberries. Halve the grapes and dice the melon. Peel and segment the orange, then chop it into bite-sized pieces.

Step 2: Make the Citrus Dressing
1. In a small bowl, whisk together the orange juice, lemon juice, honey, orange zest, and olive oil (if using). Adjust sweetness to taste.

Step 3: Assemble the Salad
1. In a large mixing bowl, combine the prepared fruits.
2. Drizzle the citrus dressing over the fruit mixture.
3. Gently toss to coat the fruits evenly with the dressing.

Step 4: Add the Mint
1. Sprinkle the chopped mint leaves over the salad. Toss lightly to combine.

Serving Suggestions
- Serve immediately for the freshest flavor and texture.
- Pair with a dollop of Greek yogurt for a creamy element.
- Enjoy as a refreshing side dish with grilled fish or chicken.

This **Fresh Fruit Salad with Mint and Citrus Dressing** showcases the simplicity and healthfulness of the Mediterranean Diet. Packed with vitamins, fiber, and antioxidants, it's a delightful way to nourish your body and delight your taste buds. Enjoy the vibrant flavors and textures of this Mediterranean-inspired treat!

1. Classic Hummus with a Paprika Olive Oil Swirl

Yield: 2 servings | **Preparation Time:** 10 minutes | **Cooking Time:** None (if using canned chickpeas)

Ingredients	Nutritional Information (Per Serving)
Base Ingredients • 1 cup canned chickpeas, drained and rinsed • 2 tbsp tahini (sesame seed paste) • 2 tbsp freshly squeezed lemon juice • 1 clove garlic, minced • 2 tbsp extra virgin olive oil, divided • 1/4 tsp sea salt (or to taste) • 1/4 tsp ground cumin • 2–3 tbsp water (adjust for desired consistency) **For the Swirl** • 1/2 tsp sweet paprika • 1 tbsp extra virgin olive oil **Optional Customizations** • Add a pinch of cayenne for heat. • Substitute sweet paprika with smoked paprika for a deeper flavor. • Top with toasted pine nuts or a sprinkle of za'atar for added texture and flavor.	• **Calories:** 190 kcal • **Protein:** 5 g • **Carbohydrates:** 12 g • **Fats:** 13 g • **Fiber:** 4 g • **Cholesterol:** 0 mg • **Sodium:** 180 mg • **Potassium:** 170 mg

Equipment Needed
- Food processor or high-speed blender
- Small mixing bowl
- Spoon for swirling

Step-by-Step Instructions
Step 1: Blend the Hummus
1. Place the chickpeas, tahini, lemon juice, garlic, 1 tablespoon of olive oil, sea salt, and cumin in a food processor.
2. Blend until smooth, stopping to scrape down the sides as needed.
3. Gradually add water, 1 tablespoon at a time, until the hummus reaches your desired creamy consistency.

Step 2: Prepare the Paprika Olive Oil
1. combine the remaining olive oil and paprika in a small mixing bowl.
2. Stir until the paprika is evenly mixed with the oil.

Step 3: Serve the Hummus
1. Transfer the hummus to a shallow serving bowl.
2. Use the back of a spoon to create a small well or swirl pattern in the center of the hummus.
3. Pour the paprika olive oil mixture into the well or along the swirl.

Serving Suggestions
- Serve with warm whole-grain pita bread, fresh vegetable sticks (cucumbers, bell peppers), or crispy pita chips.
- Pair with a side of olives and pickled vegetables for a complete Mediterranean snack platter.
- Use as a spread for sandwiches or wraps.

---

2. Crispy Baked Zucchini Fries with Garlic Yogurt Dip

Yield: 2 servings | **Preparation Time:** 15 minutes | **Cooking Time:** 20 minutes

Ingredients	Nutritional Information (Per Serving)
For the Zucchini Fries • 1 medium zucchini • 1/3 cup whole wheat breadcrumbs (or almond flour for gluten-free) • 2 tbsp grated Parmesan cheese (optional) • 1/4 tsp garlic powder • 1/4 tsp smoked paprika • 1/4 tsp sea salt • 1/8 tsp ground black pepper • 1 large egg **For the Garlic Yogurt Dip** • 1/2 cup plain Greek yogurt • 1 small clove garlic, minced • 1 tbsp fresh lemon juice • 1 tbsp extra virgin olive oil • 1 tbsp fresh parsley, finely chopped • 1/4 tsp sea salt **Optional Customizations** • Add dried oregano or thyme to the breadcrumb mixture for extra flavor. • Substitute the Parmesan with nutritional yeast for a dairy-free option.	• **Calories:** 210 kcal • **Protein:** 10 g • **Carbohydrates:** 18 g • **Fats:** 11 g • **Fiber:** 3 g • **Cholesterol:** 75 mg • **Sodium:** 320 mg • **Potassium:** 400 mg

. **Equipment Needed**
- Baking sheet
- Parchment paper
- Small mixing bowls
- Whisk
- Knife and cutting board

Step-by-Step Instructions
Step 1: Preheat the Oven
1. Preheat your oven to 425°F (220°C).
2. Line a baking sheet with parchment paper.

Step 2: Prepare the Zucchini
1. Wash and dry the zucchini. Cut it into sticks approximately 1/2 inch thick and 3 inches long.

Step 3: Prepare the Breading Station
1. In a small bowl, whisk the egg.
2. In another bowl, combine the breadcrumbs, Parmesan cheese (if using), garlic powder, smoked paprika, sea salt, and black pepper.

Step 4: Coat the Zucchini Sticks
1. Dip each zucchini stick into the egg, allowing any excess to drip off.
2. Roll the stick in the breadcrumb mixture, pressing gently to ensure an even coating.
3. Place the coated zucchini sticks on the prepared baking sheet, leaving space between each one.

Step 5: Bake the Zucchini Fries
1. Bake in the preheated oven for 15–20 minutes, turning once halfway through, until golden brown and crispy.

Step 6: Prepare the Garlic Yogurt Dip
1. mix the Greek yogurt, minced garlic, lemon juice, olive oil, parsley, and sea salt in a small bowl.
2. Stir until smooth and well combined.

Serving Suggestions

- Serve the zucchini fries warm with the garlic yogurt dip on the side.
- Pair with a light Mediterranean salad for a complete meal.
- Add a sprinkle of fresh herbs like parsley or dill for garnish.

This **Crispy Baked Zucchini Fries with Garlic Yogurt Dip** is a delicious and nutritious snack that showcases the wholesome ingredients and vibrant flavors of the Mediterranean Diet. It's rich in fiber, heart-healthy fats, and protein, making it a satisfying treat for any occasion. Enjoy!

3. Stuffed Grape Leaves with Lemon Herb Sauce

Yield: 2 servings (approximately 10 grape leaves) | **Preparation Time:** 25 minutes | **Cooking Time:** 35 minutes

Ingredients	Nutritional Information (Per Serving)
For the Grape Leaves • 10 grape leaves (jarred or fresh, rinsed and patted dry) • 1/4 cup uncooked short-grain rice (e.g., arborio) • 2 tbsp diced onion • 2 tbsp diced tomatoes • 1 tbsp fresh parsley, finely chopped • 1 tbsp fresh dill, finely chopped • 1 tbsp fresh mint, finely chopped • 1 tbsp extra virgin olive oil • 1/4 tsp ground black pepper • 1/4 tsp sea salt **For the Lemon Herb Sauce** • 2 tbsp fresh lemon juice • 1/4 cup vegetable or chicken broth • 1 tbsp extra virgin olive oil • 1/2 tsp garlic, minced • 1 tsp fresh parsley, finely chopped • 1/4 tsp dried oregano **Optional Customizations** • Add 2 tbsp pine nuts or currants to the rice mixture for extra texture and sweetness. • Substitute quinoa for rice for a higher protein content.	• **Calories:** 180 kcal • **Protein:** 4 g • **Carbohydrates:** 22 g • **Fats:** 8 g • **Fiber:** 3 g • **Cholesterol:** 0 mg • **Sodium:** 220 mg • **Potassium:** 250 mg

Equipment Needed
- Medium saucepan with lid
- Mixing bowls
- Small baking dish or skillet

Step-by-Step Instructions
Step 1: Prepare the Rice Filling
1. In a mixing bowl, combine the uncooked rice, onion, tomatoes, parsley, dill, mint, olive oil, salt, and pepper. Mix until well combined.

Step 2: Stuff the Grape Leaves
1. Lay a grape leaf shiny side down on a flat surface.
2. Place about 1 tablespoon of the rice mixture at the base of the leaf.
3. Fold in the sides, then roll tightly from the base to the tip to form a small cylinder. Repeat with the remaining grape leaves.

Step 3: Arrange and Cook
1. Line the bottom of a small baking dish or skillet with a few grape leaves to prevent sticking.
2. Arrange the stuffed grape leaves seam-side down in a single layer.
3. In a small bowl, mix the lemon juice, broth, olive oil, garlic, parsley, and oregano to create the sauce.
4. Pour the sauce over the grape leaves, ensuring they are partially submerged.
5. Cover the dish with a lid or aluminum foil.

Step 4: Simmer
1. Place the dish over low to medium heat and simmer for 30–35 minutes, or until the rice is tender and the flavors are infused.

Step 5: Serve
1. Transfer the grape leaves to a serving plate. Drizzle with any remaining sauce from the pan and garnish with extra parsley or lemon wedges.

Serving Suggestions

- Serve as an appetizer or alongside a Mediterranean platter with hummus, olives, and pita bread.
- Pair with a simple cucumber and yogurt salad for a refreshing contrast.
- Enjoy warm or at room temperature.

---

4. Marinated Olives and Feta Cheese Platter

Yield: 2 servings | **Preparation Time:** 10 minutes | **Cooking Time:** None

Ingredients	Nutritional Information (Per Serving)
Base Ingredients • 1/2 cup mixed olives (green, black, or Kalamata) • 1/4 cup feta cheese, cubed • 2 tbsp extra virgin olive oil • 1 tsp lemon zest • 1 tbsp fresh lemon juice • 1 clove garlic, minced • 1 tsp dried oregano • 1 tsp fresh thyme leaves (or 1/2 tsp dried thyme) • 1/4 tsp red chili flakes (optional, for heat) **Optional Customizations** • Add 1 tbsp chopped roasted red peppers for sweetness. • Include 1 tbsp toasted pine nuts for extra crunch. • Substitute lemon zest with orange zest for a unique citrus note.	• **Calories:** 180 kcal • **Protein:** 4 g • **Carbohydrates:** 3 g • **Fats:** 18 g • **Fiber:** 1 g • **Cholesterol:** 15 mg • **Sodium:** 600 mg • **Potassium:** 90 mg

Equipment Needed

- Small mixing bowl
- Serving platter or shallow dish

Step-by-Step Instructions

Step 1: Prepare the Marinade

1. In a small mixing bowl, whisk together the olive oil, lemon zest, lemon juice, minced garlic, oregano, thyme, and red chili flakes (if using).

Step 2: Marinate the Olives and Feta

1. Add the mixed olives and feta cubes to the bowl with the marinade. Toss gently to coat, ensuring the flavors are evenly distributed.

Step 3: Rest for Flavor

1. Allow the mixture to sit at room temperature for at least 10 minutes for the flavors to meld. For deeper flavor, cover and refrigerate for up to 1 hour. Bring to room temperature before serving.

Step 4: Assemble the Platter

1. Transfer the marinated olives and feta to a shallow dish or serving platter. Drizzle any remaining marinade over the top for extra flavor.

Serving Suggestions

- Pair with whole-grain crackers, crusty bread, or pita chips for dipping.
- Serve alongside fresh vegetables like cucumber slices and cherry tomatoes for a refreshing contrast.
- Include as part of a more enormous Mediterranean platter with hummus, roasted nuts, and stuffed grape leaves.

This **Marinated Olives and Feta Cheese Platter** is a perfect example of the Mediterranean Diet's focus on bold flavors, heart-healthy fats, and simple preparation. It's a versatile and satisfying dish, whether enjoyed as a snack, appetizer, or part of a larger meal. Bon appétit!

5. Roasted Red Pepper and Walnut Spread (Muhammara)

Yield: 2 servings | **Preparation Time:** 10 minutes | **Cooking Time:** 10 minutes (if roasting peppers at home)

Ingredients	Nutritional Information (Per Serving)
Base Ingredients • 1 cup roasted red peppers (jarred or homemade) • 1/2 cup walnuts, lightly toasted • 1 small garlic clove, minced • 2 tbsp olive oil • 1 tbsp pomegranate molasses (or 1 tsp honey for a substitute) • 1 tbsp fresh lemon juice • 1/2 tsp ground cumin • 1/2 tsp smoked paprika • 1/4 tsp sea salt (or to taste) • 1/8 tsp cayenne pepper (optional, for heat) **Optional Customizations** • Add 1/4 cup breadcrumbs for a thicker texture. • Substitute walnuts with almonds or pine nuts for a different nutty flavor. • Sprinkle with fresh parsley or mint for a fresh garnish.	• **Calories:** 200 kcal • **Protein:** 4 g • **Carbohydrates:** 8 g • **Fats:** 18 g • **Fiber:** 2 g • **Cholesterol:** 0 mg • **Sodium:** 200 mg • **Potassium:** 230 mg

Equipment Needed
- Food processor or blender
- Skillet (for toasting walnuts, if needed)

Step-by-Step Instructions
Step 1: Toast the Walnuts
1. If using raw walnuts, toast them in a dry skillet over medium heat for 3–4 minutes, stirring frequently, until lightly browned and fragrant. Set aside to cool.

Step 2: Blend the Ingredients
1. In a food processor or blender, combine the roasted red peppers, toasted walnuts, garlic, olive oil, pomegranate molasses, lemon juice, cumin, smoked paprika, sea salt, and cayenne pepper (if using).
2. Blend until smooth but slightly chunky, depending on your preference.

Step 3: Adjust Seasoning and Texture
1. Taste the spread and adjust the seasoning with more salt or lemon juice as needed.
2. If the mixture is too thick, add olive oil or water to reach your desired consistency.

Step 4: Serve or Store
1. Transfer the muhammara to a serving bowl and drizzle with olive oil for a glossy finish.
2. Garnish with a sprinkle of chopped walnuts, pomegranate seeds, or fresh parsley, if desired.

Serving Suggestions
- Serve with warm pita bread, whole-grain crackers, or fresh vegetable sticks (e.g., cucumbers, carrots).
- Use it as a flavorful sandwich spread or a topping for grilled fish or chicken.
- Pair with a Mediterranean mezze platter featuring hummus, olives, and stuffed grape leaves.

This **Roasted Red Pepper and Walnut Spread (Muhammara)** is a deliciously versatile dish that highlights the rich flavors and healthy ingredients of the Mediterranean Diet. Packed with heart-healthy fats, antioxidants, and a hint of spice, it's an irresistible addition to any meal or gathering. Enjoy!

6. Mini Spinach and Cheese Phyllo Pies

Yield: 2 servings (6 mini pies) | **Preparation Time:** 20 minutes | **Cooking Time:** 25 minutes

Ingredients	Nutritional Information (Per Serving)
Base Ingredients • 6 sheets phyllo dough, thawed if frozen • 2 tbsp extra virgin olive oil (for brushing) • 1 cup fresh spinach, finely chopped • 1/4 cup feta cheese, crumbled • 1/4 cup ricotta cheese • 1 small egg, lightly beaten • 1 tbsp fresh dill, finely chopped • 1 tbsp fresh parsley, finely chopped • 1/4 tsp ground nutmeg (optional) • 1/4 tsp ground black pepper • 1/8 tsp sea salt (adjust based on the saltiness of the feta) **Optional Customizations** • Substitute feta cheese with goat cheese or Parmesan for a different flavor profile. • Add 1 tbsp pine nuts for a nutty crunch. • Include 1/4 cup chopped mushrooms or leeks for additional texture and flavor.	• **Calories:** 250 kcal • **Protein:** 8 g • **Carbohydrates:** 16 g • **Fats:** 16 g • **Fiber:** 2 g • **Cholesterol:** 70 mg • **Sodium:** 350 mg • **Potassium:** 200 mg

Equipment Needed

- Baking sheet
- Parchment paper or non-stick spray
- Small mixing bowl

- Pastry brush

Step-by-Step Instructions
Step 1: Prepare the Filling
1. In a small mixing bowl, combine the chopped spinach, feta cheese, ricotta cheese, beaten egg, dill, parsley, nutmeg (if using), black pepper, and salt. Mix well until evenly combined.

Step 2: Prepare the Phyllo Dough
1. Lay out the phyllo sheets on a clean surface. Cover with a damp kitchen towel to prevent drying out.
2. Brush one sheet of phyllo lightly with olive oil. Layer a second sheet on top and brush with olive oil. Repeat until you have three layers.

Step 3: Assemble the Pies
1. Cut the layered phyllo dough into 6 equal squares.
2. Place a heaping tablespoon of the spinach and cheese mixture in the center of each square.
3. Fold each square into a triangle or bundle, pinching or twisting the edges to seal. Brush the tops with olive oil for a golden finish.

Step 4: Bake the Pies
1. Preheat the oven to 375°F (190°C).
2. Line a baking sheet with parchment paper or lightly grease it.
3. Arrange the assembled pies on the baking sheet and bake for 20–25 minutes or until the phyllo is golden brown and crispy.

Step 5: Cool and Serve
1. Remove the pies from the oven and let them cool slightly before serving.

Serving Suggestions
- Serve warm with a side of tzatziki or a simple cucumber and tomato salad.
- Pair with a bowl of lentil soup or a light green salad for a complete meal.
- Enjoy as a snack or appetizer alongside a platter of olives and hummus.

7. Bruschetta with Heirloom Tomatoes and Basil

Yield: 2 servings (4 slices) | **Preparation Time:** 10 minutes | **Cooking Time:** 5 minutes

Ingredients	Nutritional Information (Per Serving)
Base Ingredients • 4 slices whole-grain or sourdough bread • 1 cup diced heirloom tomatoes (mixed colors for vibrancy) • 2 tbsp extra virgin olive oil, divided • 1 tbsp balsamic vinegar • 1/4 cup fresh basil leaves, thinly sliced • 1 clove garlic, halved • 1/4 tsp sea salt (or to taste) • 1/8 tsp ground black pepper **Optional Customizations** • Add a sprinkle of grated Parmesan or crumbled feta for extra richness. • Substitute balsamic vinegar with red wine vinegar for a sharper flavor. • Include a pinch of red chili flakes for a hint of heat.	• **Calories:** 200 kcal • **Protein:** 6 g • **Carbohydrates:** 20 g • **Fats:** 10 g • **Fiber:** 3 g • **Cholesterol:** 0 mg • **Sodium:** 220 mg • **Potassium:** 250 mg

Equipment Needed
- Grill pan or toaster (for toasting bread)
- Mixing bowl
- Spoon for assembling

Step-by-Step Instructions

Step 1: Prepare the Tomato Topping
1. Mix the diced heirloom tomatoes, 1 tablespoon of olive oil, balsamic vinegar, sliced basil, sea salt, and black pepper in a mixing bowl.
2. Stir gently to combine, and let the mixture sit for 5 minutes to allow the flavors to meld.

Step 2: Toast the Bread
1. Lightly brush each slice of bread with the remaining olive oil.
2. Toast the bread on a grill pan over medium heat for 1–2 minutes on each side until golden and crispy, or use a toaster.

Step 3: Rub with Garlic
1. While the bread is still warm, rub one side of each slice with the cut side of the garlic clove. This infuses the bread with a subtle garlic flavor.

Step 4: Assemble the Bruschetta
1. Spoon the tomato mixture onto the toasted bread slices, dividing it evenly.
2. Drizzle any remaining liquid from the bowl over the assembled bruschetta for added flavor.

Serving Suggestions
- Serve as an appetizer or light snack alongside olives and a simple green salad.
- Pair with a glass of white wine or sparkling water with lemon for a refreshing combination.
- Enjoy as a side dish with grilled chicken, fish, or pasta.

1. Classic Greek Salad with Kalamata Olives and Feta

Yield: 2 servings | **Preparation Time:** 10 minutes | **Cooking Time:** None

Ingredients	Nutritional Information (Per Serving)
Base Ingredients • 2 cups chopped romaine lettuce • 1 cup cherry tomatoes, halved • 1 medium cucumber, sliced into half-moons • 1/2 red onion, thinly sliced • 1/2 green bell pepper, sliced • 1/4 cup Kalamata olives, pitted • 1/4 cup feta cheese, crumbled or cubed **For the Dressing** • 3 tbsp extra virgin olive oil • 1 tbsp red wine vinegar • 1/2 tsp dried oregano • 1/8 tsp ground black pepper **Optional Customizations** • Add 1/4 tsp Dijon mustard to the dressing for a slight tang. • Substitute green bell pepper with roasted red peppers for a sweeter flavor.	• **Calories:** 180 kcal • **Protein:** 5 g • **Carbohydrates:** 10 g • **Fats:** 14 g • **Fiber:** 3 g • **Cholesterol:** 15 mg • **Sodium:** 420 mg • **Potassium:** 350 mg

Equipment Needed

- Large mixing bowl
- Small bowl or jar (for dressing)
- Whisk or fork

Step-by-Step Instructions

Step 1: Prepare the Vegetables

1. Wash all the vegetables thoroughly.
2. Chop the romaine lettuce (if using) and place it in a large mixing bowl.
3. Add the cherry tomatoes, cucumber slices, red onion, green bell pepper, and Kalamata olives.

Step 2: Make the Dressing

1. In a small bowl or jar, whisk together the olive oil, red wine vinegar, oregano, sea salt, black pepper, and minced garlic until emulsified.

Step 3: Combine and Toss

1. Pour the dressing over the salad and toss gently to coat the vegetables evenly.

Step 4: Add the Feta Cheese

1. Top the salad with crumbled or cubed feta cheese.

Serving Suggestions

- Serve as a starter or side dish with grilled fish, chicken, or lamb.
- Pair with whole-grain pita bread and hummus for a light Mediterranean meal.
- Enjoy a refreshing lunch with a small bowl of lentil soup.

---

2. Mediterranean Quinoa Salad with Cucumber and Parsley

Yield: 2 servings | **Preparation Time:** 10 minutes | **Cooking Time:** 15 minutes

Ingredients	Nutritional Information (Per Serving)
Base Ingredients • 1/2 cup quinoa, rinsed • 1 cup water • 1/2 medium cucumber, diced • 1/2 cup cherry tomatoes, halved • 2 tbsp red onion, finely chopped • 1/4 cup fresh parsley, finely chopped • 2 tbsp Kalamata olives, sliced • 2 tbsp crumbled feta cheese (optional) **For the Dressing** • 2 tbsp extra virgin olive oil • 1 tbsp fresh lemon juice • 1/2 tsp lemon zest • 1/4 tsp dried oregano • 1/4 tsp sea salt (or to taste) • 1/8 tsp ground black pepper **Optional Customizations** • Add 1/4 cup cooked chickpeas for added protein. • Include 1 tbsp chopped fresh mint for a refreshing twist.	• **Calories:** 220 kcal • **Protein:** 6 g • **Carbohydrates:** 20 g • **Fats:** 12 g • **Fiber:** 4 g • **Cholesterol:** 0 mg (with feta: 10 mg) • **Sodium:** 240 mg • **Potassium:** 310 mg

Equipment Needed
- Medium saucepan with lid
- Large mixing bowl
- Small whisk or fork

Step-by-Step Instructions

Step 1: Cook the Quinoa
1. In a medium saucepan, combine the quinoa and water.
2. Bring to a boil, reduce the heat to low, cover, and simmer for 15 minutes until the quinoa is tender and water is absorbed.
3. Remove from heat and let stand, covered, for 5 minutes. Fluff with a fork and set aside to cool.

Step 2: Prepare the Vegetables
1. While the quinoa is cooked, dice the cucumber, halve the cherry tomatoes, and chop the parsley and red onion.

Step 3: Make the Dressing
1. In a small bowl, whisk together the olive oil, lemon juice, lemon zest, oregano, sea salt, and black pepper until emulsified.

Step 4: Assemble the Salad
1. combine the cooked quinoa, cucumber, cherry tomatoes, red onion, parsley, and Kalamata olives in a large mixing bowl.
2. Pour the dressing over the salad and toss gently to coat all ingredients evenly.

Step 5: Add Finishing Touches
1. Top with crumbled feta cheese, if using.

Serving Suggestions
- Serve as a light lunch with pita bread and hummus.
- Pair with grilled chicken or fish for a complete Mediterranean-inspired meal.
- Enjoy as a refreshing picnic or potluck dish.

3. Roasted Beet and Arugula Salad with Citrus Vinaigrette

Yield: 2 servings | **Preparation Time:** 10 minutes | **Cooking Time:** 40 minutes

Ingredients	Nutritional Information (Per Serving)
Base Ingredients • 2 medium beets • 2 cups fresh arugula • 1/4 cup crumbled feta cheese (optional) • 2 tbsp chopped walnuts, toasted • 1/2 orange, segmented • 1/4 small red onion, thinly sliced **For the Citrus Vinaigrette** • 2 tbsp extra virgin olive oil • 1 tbsp freshly squeezed orange juice • 1 tbsp freshly squeezed lemon juice • 1 tsp honey or maple syrup • 1/4 tsp Dijon mustard • 1/4 tsp sea salt • 1/8 tsp ground black pepper **Optional Customizations** • Add a handful of pomegranate seeds for extra sweetness and texture. • Substitute walnuts with pistachios or almonds for a different nutty flavor. • Include 1 tsp fresh dill or parsley for an herbal note.	• **Calories:** 220 kcal • **Protein:** 6 g • **Carbohydrates:** 18 g • **Fats:** 14 g • **Fiber:** 5 g • **Cholesterol:** 10 mg (with feta) • **Sodium:** 200 mg • **Potassium:** 350 mg

Equipment Needed
- Baking sheet
- Aluminum foil
- Small whisk or fork
- Mixing bowls

Step-by-Step Instructions

Step 1: Roast the Beets
1. Preheat the oven to 400°F (200°C).
2. Wash the beets thoroughly, trim the tops, and wrap each beet in aluminum foil.
3. Place the wrapped beets on a baking sheet and roast for 40 minutes or until tender when pierced with a knife.
4. Let the beets cool slightly, then peel off the skin and slice into wedges or cubes.

Step 2: Prepare the Vinaigrette
1. In a small bowl, whisk together the olive oil, orange juice, lemon juice, honey, Dijon mustard, sea salt, and black pepper until emulsified.

Step 3: Assemble the Salad
1. In a large mixing bowl, combine the arugula, roasted beets, orange segments, and red onion.
2. Drizzle the citrus vinaigrette over the salad and toss gently to coat.

Step 4: Add the Toppings
1. Top the salad with crumbled feta cheese (if using) and toasted walnuts.

Serving Suggestions
- Serve as a refreshing appetizer or a light main course with a slice of whole-grain bread.
- Pair with grilled fish or chicken for a complete Mediterranean-inspired meal.
- Enjoy as a side dish alongside lentil soup or hummus.

4. Warm Lentil Salad with Sun-Dried Tomatoes and Goat Cheese

Yield: 2 servings | **Preparation Time:** 10 minutes | **Cooking Time:** 25 minutes

Ingredients	Nutritional Information (Per Serving)
Base Ingredients • 1/2 cup dried green or brown lentils, rinsed • 1 1/4 cups water or vegetable broth • 1/4 cup sun-dried tomatoes (packed in olive oil), chopped • 1/4 cup crumbled goat cheese • 2 tbsp extra virgin olive oil (divided) • 1/4 cup red onion, finely chopped • 1 small clove garlic, minced • 1 tbsp fresh parsley, chopped • 1 tbsp fresh basil, chopped • 1 tbsp balsamic vinegar • 1/4 tsp sea salt (or to taste) • 1/8 tsp ground black pepper **Optional Customizations** • Add 1/4 cup toasted walnuts for crunch. • Substitute goat cheese with feta for a saltier flavor. • Include 1/4 cup roasted red peppers for added sweetness	• **Calories:** 280 kcal • **Protein:** 10 g • **Carbohydrates:** 30 g • **Fats:** 12 g • **Fiber:** 10 g • **Cholesterol:** 10 mg • **Sodium:** 220 mg • **Potassium:** 450 mg

Equipment Needed
- Medium saucepan
- Small skillet
- Mixing bowl

Step-by-Step Instructions

Step 1: Cook the Lentils
1. combine the lentils and water or vegetable broth in a medium saucepan. Bring to a boil over medium-high heat.
2. Reduce the heat to low, cover, and simmer for 20–25 minutes or until the lentils are tender but not mushy. Drain any excess liquid and set aside.

Step 2: Prepare the Aromatics
1. heat 1 tablespoon of olive oil in a small skillet over medium heat while the lentils cook.
2. Add the red onion and garlic, sautéing for 2–3 minutes until softened and fragrant.

Step 3: Combine the Salad
1. combine the cooked lentils, sautéed onion and garlic, chopped sun-dried tomatoes, parsley, and basil in a large mixing bowl.
2. Drizzle with the remaining olive oil and balsamic vinegar. Toss gently to coat.

Step 4: Add the Goat Cheese
1. Sprinkle the crumbled goat cheese over the lentil mixture and gently fold it in, allowing the warmth of the lentils to slightly soften the cheese.

Serving Suggestions
- Serve warm as a main dish with a slice of crusty whole-grain bread.
- Pair with a simple green salad for a balanced Mediterranean meal.
- Enjoy as a hearty side dish with grilled chicken or fish.

5. Chickpea and Avocado Salad with Lemon Garlic Dressing

Yield: 2 servings | **Preparation Time:** 10 minutes | **Cooking Time:** None

Ingredients	Nutritional Information (Per Serving)
Base Ingredients • 1 cup cooked chickpeas (or 1 can, drained and rinsed) • 1 ripe avocado, diced • 1/2 cup cherry tomatoes, halved • 1/4 cup cucumber, diced • 2 tbsp red onion, finely chopped • 2 tbsp fresh parsley, chopped • 2 tbsp fresh cilantro or mint, chopped (optional) **For the Lemon Garlic Dressing** • 2 tbsp extra virgin olive oil • 1 tbsp freshly squeezed lemon juice • 1 small clove garlic, minced • 1/4 tsp sea salt (or to taste) • 1/8 tsp ground black pepper • 1/4 tsp ground cumin (optional for extra flavor) **Optional Customizations** • Add 1 tbsp crumbled feta cheese for a creamy, tangy element. • Include 1/4 tsp red chili flakes for a spicy kick. • Add 1/4 cup roasted red peppers or olives for more Mediterranean flair.	• **Calories:** 290 kcal • **Protein:** 8 g • **Carbohydrates:** 25 g • **Fats:** 18 g • **Fiber:** 10 g • **Cholesterol:** 0 mg • **Sodium:** 200 mg • **Potassium:** 580 mg

Equipment Needed
- Mixing bowl
- Small whisk or fork

Step-by-Step Instructions
Step 1: Prepare the Vegetables and Chickpeas
1. Drain and rinse the chickpeas if using canned.
2. Dice the avocado, cherry tomatoes, cucumber, and red onion.

Step 2: Make the Dressing
1. In a small bowl, whisk together the olive oil, lemon juice, minced garlic, sea salt, black pepper, and cumin (if using).

Step 3: Combine the Salad
1. In a large mixing bowl, combine the chickpeas, avocado, cherry tomatoes, cucumber, red onion, parsley, and cilantro or mint (if using).
2. Pour the lemon garlic dressing over the salad and toss gently to evenly coat all ingredients.

Serving Suggestions
- Serve as a light lunch with a slice of whole-grain bread or pita.
- Pair with grilled fish, chicken, or tofu for a complete Mediterranean-inspired meal.
- Enjoy as a refreshing side dish alongside hummus and olives.

This **Chickpea and Avocado Salad with Lemon Garlic Dressing** is a perfect example of the Mediterranean Diet's emphasis on fresh, wholesome ingredients. Packed with fiber, healthy fats, and vibrant flavors, it's a satisfying and nourishing dish for any occasion. Enjoy!

6. Caprese Salad with Balsamic Glaze and Fresh Basil

Yield: 2 servings | **Preparation Time:** 10 minutes | **Cooking Time:** None

Ingredients	Nutritional Information (Per Serving)
Base Ingredients <ul><li>2 medium ripe tomatoes, sliced</li><li>4 oz fresh mozzarella, sliced</li><li>1/4 cup fresh basil leaves</li><li>2 tbsp balsamic glaze</li><li>1 tbsp extra virgin olive oil</li><li>1/4 tsp sea salt (or to taste)</li><li>1/8 tsp ground black pepper</li></ul> **Optional Customizations** <ul><li>Add a sprinkle of red chili flakes for a touch of heat.</li><li>Use heirloom tomatoes for a colorful and flavorful variation.</li><li>Substitute mozzarella with burrata for a creamier texture.</li></ul>	<ul><li>**Calories:** 230 kcal</li><li>**Protein:** 10 g</li><li>**Carbohydrates:** 8 g</li><li>**Fats:** 18 g</li><li>**Fiber:** 1 g</li><li>**Cholesterol:** 25 mg</li><li>**Sodium:** 250 mg</li><li>**Potassium:** 400 mg</li></ul>

Equipment Needed
- Sharp knife and cutting board
- Serving platter or plate

Step-by-Step Instructions
Step 1: Slice the Ingredients
1. Slice the tomatoes and mozzarella into 1/4-inch-thick rounds.

Step 2: Arrange the Salad
1. On a serving platter, alternate tomato, mozzarella, and fresh basil leaves overlap.

Step 3: Season and Dress
1. Drizzle the olive oil evenly over the arranged slices.
2. Season with sea salt and black pepper to taste.
3. Drizzle the balsamic glaze in a decorative pattern over the top of the salad.

Step 4: Garnish and Serve
1. Add a few additional basil leaves to garnish.
2. Serve immediately for the freshest flavor and texture.

Serving Suggestions
- Serve as an appetizer or side dish with grilled chicken, fish, or pasta.
- Pair with a slice of crusty whole-grain bread to soak up the delicious juices.
- Enjoy a light lunch with a glass of sparkling water or wine.

This **Caprese Salad with Balsamic Glaze and Fresh Basil** showcases the beauty of Mediterranean cuisine, emphasizing simple, fresh ingredients. Packed with healthy fats, protein, and vibrant flavors, it's a delicious and wholesome dish for any occasion. Enjoy!

7. Pomegranate and Spinach Salad with Toasted Almonds

Yield: 2 servings | **Preparation Time:** 10 minutes | **Cooking Time:** 5 minutes

Ingredients	Nutritional Information (Per Serving)
Base Ingredients • 4 cups fresh baby spinach • 1/2 cup pomegranate arils • 2 tbsp sliced almonds, toasted • 2 tbsp crumbled feta cheese (optional) **For the Dressing** • 2 tbsp extra virgin olive oil • 1 tbsp pomegranate juice (or fresh orange juice) • 1 tbsp balsamic vinegar • 1 tsp honey or maple syrup • 1/4 tsp sea salt (or to taste) • 1/8 tsp ground black pepper **Optional Customizations** • Add 1/4 cup thinly sliced red onion for a bit of sharpness. • Include 1 tbsp dried cranberries for extra sweetness. • Substitute almonds with walnuts or pecans for a different nutty flavor.	• **Calories:** 200 kcal • **Protein:** 4 g • **Carbohydrates:** 15 g • **Fats:** 14 g • **Fiber:** 4 g • **Cholesterol:** 0 mg (with feta: 10 mg) • **Sodium:** 200 mg • **Potassium:** 400 mg

Equipment Needed

• Medium mixing bowl
• Small skillet (for toasting almonds)
• Small whisk or fork

Step-by-Step Instructions

Step 1: Toast the Almonds

1. Heat a small skillet over medium heat.
2. Add the sliced almonds and toast for 2–3 minutes, stirring frequently, until golden and fragrant. Remove from heat and set aside to cool.

Step 2: Prepare the Dressing

1. In a small bowl, whisk together the olive oil, pomegranate juice, balsamic vinegar, honey, sea salt, and black pepper until emulsified.

Step 3: Assemble the Salad

1. Mix the spinach, pomegranate arils, and toasted almonds in a medium mixing bowl.
2. Drizzle the dressing over the salad and toss gently to evenly coat all ingredients.

Step 4: Add the Finishing Touches

1. Sprinkle the crumbled feta cheese on top if using.

Serving Suggestions

- Serve as a starter or side dish with grilled chicken, fish, or tofu.
- Pair with a slice of whole-grain bread or pita for a light Mediterranean-inspired meal.
- Enjoy a refreshing lunch with a bowl of lentil soup or hummus.

This **Pomegranate and Spinach Salad with Toasted Almonds** is a beautiful and nutritious dish highlighting the Mediterranean Diet's focus on fresh, wholesome ingredients. Packed with antioxidants, healthy fats, and vibrant flavors, it's a delicious way to nourish your body and delight your taste buds. Enjoy!

1. Lemon Herb Couscous with Chickpeas and Pine Nuts

Yield: 2 servings | **Preparation Time**: 10 minutes | **Cooking Time**: 10 minutes

Ingredients	Nutritional Information (Per Serving)
Base Ingredients • 1/2 cup couscous • 3/4 cup vegetable broth or water • 1/2 cup cooked chickpeas (or canned, drained and rinsed) • 2 tbsp pine nuts, toasted • 2 tbsp fresh parsley, chopped • 1 tbsp fresh mint, chopped • 1 tbsp extra virgin olive oil • 1 tbsp fresh lemon juice • 1/2 tsp lemon zest • 1/4 tsp ground cumin **Optional Customizations** • Add 1/4 cup diced cucumber or cherry tomatoes for extra freshness. • Include 1 tbsp crumbled feta cheese for added richness. • Substitute pine nuts with slivered almonds or chopped walnuts.	• **Calories:** 250 kcal • **Protein:** 8 g • **Carbohydrates:** 35 g • **Fats:** 9 g • **Fiber:** 6 g • **Cholesterol:** 0 mg • **Sodium:** 200 mg • **Potassium:** 250 mg

Equipment Needed
- Medium saucepan with lid
- Small skillet (for toasting pine nuts)
- Fork (for fluffing couscous)
- Mixing bowl

Step-by-Step Instructions

Step 1: Cook the Couscous
1. bring the vegetable broth or water to a boil in a medium saucepan.
2. Stir in the couscous, cover, and remove from heat. Let it sit for 5 minutes, then fluff with a fork to separate the grains.

Step 2: Toast the Pine Nuts
1. heat a small skillet over medium heat while the couscous is cooking.
2. Add the pine nuts and toast for 2–3 minutes, stirring frequently, until golden and fragrant. Remove from heat and set aside.

Step 3: Combine the Ingredients
1. combine the cooked couscous, chickpeas, parsley, mint, and toasted pine nuts in a large mixing bowl.

Step 4: Make the Lemon Herb Dressing
1. whisk together the olive oil, lemon juice, lemon zest, cumin, sea salt, and black pepper in a small bowl.

Step 5: Toss and Serve
1. Pour the dressing over the couscous mixture and toss gently to combine.
2. Taste and adjust seasoning as needed.

Serving Suggestions
- Serve warm or room temperature as a side dish with grilled fish, chicken, or tofu.
- Pair with a simple arugula salad for a complete Mediterranean-inspired meal.
- Enjoy a light lunch with a dollop of Greek yogurt or tzatziki on the side.

2. Whole Wheat Penne with Cherry Tomatoes and Basil Pesto

Yield: 2 servings | **Preparation Time:** 10 minutes | **Cooking Time:** 15 minutes

Ingredients	Nutritional Information (Per Serving)
Base Ingredients	• **Calories:** 380 kcal
• 1 cup whole wheat penne pasta	• **Protein:** 10 g
• 1 cup cherry tomatoes, halved	• **Carbohydrates:** 52 g
• 2 tbsp olive oil, divided	• **Fats:** 14 g
• 1/4 cup basil pesto (store-bought or homemade)	• **Fiber:** 7 g
• 2 tbsp grated Parmesan cheese (optional)	• **Cholesterol:** 0 mg (with Parmesan: 10 mg)
• 2 tbsp fresh basil leaves, chopped (for garnish)	• **Sodium:** 250 mg
• 1/4 tsp sea salt (or to taste)	• **Potassium:** 320 mg
• 1/8 tsp ground black pepper	
Optional Customizations	
• Add 1/4 cup cooked chickpeas for extra protein.	
• Include 2 tbsp toasted pine nuts for a nutty crunch.	
• Substitute cherry tomatoes with sun-dried tomatoes for a more intense flavor.	

Equipment Needed
- Medium saucepan
- Skillet
- Mixing bowl

Step-by-Step Instructions

Step 1: Cook the Pasta
1. Bring a medium saucepan of salted water to a boil.
2. Add the whole wheat penne and cook according to package instructions (10–12 minutes) until al dente. Drain and set aside.

Step 2: Sauté the Cherry Tomatoes
1. Heat 1 tablespoon of olive oil in a skillet over medium heat.
2. Add the cherry tomatoes and cook for 2–3 minutes until they soften and release some juices. Season with sea salt and black pepper.

Step 3: Combine Pasta and Pesto
1. In a mixing bowl, toss the cooked penne with the basil pesto and the remaining tablespoon of olive oil until the pasta is evenly coated.

Step 4: Assemble the Dish
1. Add the sautéed cherry tomatoes to the pesto-coated pasta. Gently toss to combine.

Step 5: Garnish and Serve
1. Divide the pasta into two bowls or plates.
2. Sprinkle with grated Parmesan cheese, if desired, and garnish with fresh basil leaves.

Serving Suggestions
- Serve with a simple arugula salad drizzled with olive oil and lemon juice.
- Pair with a slice of whole-grain bread for a complete Mediterranean-inspired meal.
- Enjoy with a glass of sparkling water infused with fresh lemon or mint.

3. Mediterranean Orzo Salad with Kalamata Olives and Artichokes

Yield: 2 servings | **Preparation Time:** 10 minutes | **Cooking Time:** 10 minutes

Ingredients	Nutritional Information (Per Serving)
Base Ingredients • 1/2 cup dry orzo pasta • 1 1/4 cups water or vegetable broth • 1/4 cup Kalamata olives, pitted and halved • 1/4 cup marinated artichoke hearts, chopped • 1/4 cup cherry tomatoes, halved • 2 tbsp red onion, finely chopped • 1/4 cup fresh parsley, chopped • 1 tbsp fresh dill, chopped (optional) **For the Dressing** • 2 tbsp extra virgin olive oil • 1 tbsp freshly squeezed lemon juice • 1/2 tsp lemon zest • 1 tsp red wine vinegar • 1 small clove garlic, minced • 1/4 tsp sea salt (or to taste) • 1/8 tsp ground black pepper **Optional Customizations** • Add 2 tbsp crumbled feta cheese for a creamy element. • Include 1 tbsp capers for additional brininess. • Substitute orzo with quinoa or couscous for a gluten-free option.	• **Calories:** 260 kcal • **Protein:** 6 g • **Carbohydrates:** 30 g • **Fats:** 12 g • **Fiber:** 4 g • **Cholesterol:** 0 mg (with feta: 10 mg) • **Sodium:** 320 mg • **Potassium:** 300 mg

Equipment Needed

- Medium saucepan
- Mixing bowl
- Small whisk or fork

Step-by-Step Instructions

Step 1: Cook the Orzo

1. bring water or vegetable broth to a boil in a medium saucepan.
2. Add the orzo and cook according to package instructions (approximately 8–10 minutes) until al dente.
3. Drain and rinse with cold water to stop the cooking process. Set it aside.

Step 2: Prepare the Dressing

1. whisk together olive oil, lemon juice, lemon zest, red wine vinegar, garlic, sea salt, and black pepper until emulsified in a small bowl.

Step 3: Combine the Salad

1. In a mixing bowl, combine the cooked orzo, Kalamata olives, artichoke hearts, cherry tomatoes, red onion, parsley, and dill (if using).
2. Pour the dressing over the salad and toss gently to coat all ingredients evenly.

Step 4: Garnish and Serve

1. Taste and adjust seasoning as needed.
2. Transfer to serving plates and garnish with additional parsley or dill, if desired.

Serving Suggestions

- Serve as a side dish with grilled chicken, fish, or tofu.
- Pair with a slice of whole-grain bread or pita for a complete Mediterranean-inspired meal.
- Enjoy a light lunch with a bowl of lentil or tomato soup.

---

4. Creamy Parmesan Risotto with Sautéed Mushrooms

Yield: 2 servings | **Preparation Time**: 10 minutes | **Cooking Time**: 30 minutes

Ingredients	Nutritional Information (Per Serving)
For the Risotto	• **Calories:** 320 kcal
• 1/2 cup Arborio rice	• **Protein:** 10 g
• 2 cups low-sodium vegetable or chicken broth, warmed	• **Carbohydrates:** 38 g
• 2 tbsp extra virgin olive oil, divided	• **Fats:** 12 g
• 1/4 cup finely chopped onion	• **Fiber:** 2 g
• 1 small clove garlic, minced	• **Cholesterol:** 10 mg
• 1/4 cup dry white wine (optional)	• **Sodium:** 280 mg
• 1/4 cup grated Parmesan cheese	• **Potassium:** 350 mg
• 1 tbsp fresh parsley, chopped	
• 1/4 tsp sea salt (or to taste)	
• 1/8 tsp ground black pepper	
For the Sautéed Mushrooms	
• 1 cup cremini or button mushrooms, sliced	
• 1 tbsp extra virgin olive oil	
• 1/2 tsp fresh thyme leaves (or 1/4 tsp dried thyme)	
• 1/4 tsp sea salt	
• 1/8 tsp ground black pepper	

Optional Customizations	
• Add 1/4 cup fresh spinach to the risotto in the last 2 minutes of cooking. • Substitute Parmesan with Pecorino Romano for a sharper flavor. • Include 1 tbsp toasted pine nuts for added texture.	

Equipment Needed
- Medium saucepan
- Medium skillet
- Ladle
- Wooden spoon

Step-by-Step Instructions

Step 1: Prepare the Broth

1. Warm the vegetable or chicken broth in a medium saucepan over low heat. Keep it warm throughout the cooking process.

Step 2: Sauté the Mushrooms

1. Heat 1 tablespoon of olive oil in a skillet over medium heat.
2. Add the sliced mushrooms, thyme, sea salt, and black pepper. Sauté for 5–7 minutes until the mushrooms are golden and tender. Remove from heat and set aside.

Step 3: Cook the Risotto Base

1. In a separate medium saucepan, heat 1 tablespoon of olive oil over medium heat.
2. Add the chopped onion and cook for 2–3 minutes until translucent.
3. Stir in the garlic and cook for an additional 30 seconds.
4. Add the Arborio rice and toast for 1–2 minutes, stirring frequently.

Step 4: Add Wine (Optional) and Broth

1. Pour in the white wine (if using) and stir until fully absorbed.

2. Add the warm broth one ladle at a time, stirring frequently. Allow each ladle of broth to be absorbed before adding the next. This process takes about 18–20 minutes.

Step 5: Finish the Risotto
1. When the rice is creamy and tender but still slightly firm to the bite, remove it from heat.
2. Stir in the grated Parmesan cheese, chopped parsley, sea salt, and black pepper. Adjust seasoning as needed.

Step 6: Assemble the Dish
1. Divide the risotto between two plates or bowls.
2. If desired, Top with the sautéed mushrooms and garnish with additional parsley and Parmesan.

Serving Suggestions
- Pair with a simple arugula salad drizzled with lemon and olive oil.
- Serve alongside grilled chicken or fish for a complete Mediterranean-inspired meal.
- Enjoy with a glass of dry white wine for an elegant dining experience.

This **Creamy Parmesan Risotto with Sautéed Mushrooms** is a perfect example of the Mediterranean Diet's focus on fresh ingredients, whole grains, and healthy fats. It's a luxurious yet balanced dish that highlights the culinary richness of Mediterranean cuisine. Enjoy!

5. Barley Pilaf with Roasted Vegetables and Fresh Herbs

Yield: 2 servings | **Preparation Time:** 10 minutes | **Cooking Time:** 35 minutes

Ingredients	Nutritional Information (Per Serving)
Base Ingredients • 1/2 cup pearl barley • 1 1/4 cups low-sodium vegetable broth or water • 1/2 cup zucchini, diced. • 1/2 cup bell peppers (any color), diced. • 1/2 cup cherry tomatoes, halved. • 1/4 cup red onion, diced. • 2 tbsp extra virgin olive oil, divided. • 1/4 tsp sea salt (or to taste) • 1/8 tsp ground black pepper **For the Herb Garnish** • 2 tbsp fresh parsley, chopped. • 1 tbsp fresh dill or basil, chopped. • 1 tsp lemon zest • 1 tbsp freshly squeezed lemon juice **Optional Customizations** • Add 1/4 cup crumbled feta cheese for a tangy flavor. • Include 2 tbsp toasted pine nuts or slivered almonds for added crunch. • Substitute barley with farro or quinoa for variety.	• **Calories:** 250 kcal • **Protein:** 6 g • **Carbohydrates:** 35 g • **Fats:** 10 g • **Fiber:** 7 g • **Cholesterol:** 0 mg • **Sodium:** 150 mg • **Potassium:** 400 mg

Equipment Needed
- Medium saucepan with lid
- Baking sheet
- Mixing bowls

Step-by-Step Instructions

Step 1: Cook the Barley
1. bring the vegetable broth or water to a boil in a medium saucepan.
2. Add the barley, reduce the heat to low, cover, and simmer for 25–30 minutes or until tender and the liquid is absorbed. Set aside.

Step 2: Roast the Vegetables
1. Preheat the oven to 400°F (200°C).
2. On a baking sheet, toss the zucchini, bell peppers, cherry tomatoes, and red onion with 1 tablespoon of olive oil, sea salt, and black pepper.
3. Roast for 15–20 minutes, stirring once halfway through, until the vegetables are tender and slightly caramelized.

Step 3: Combine the Pilaf
1. combine the cooked barley and roasted vegetables in a large mixing bowl.
2. Drizzle with 1 tablespoon of olive oil and the lemon juice. Add the lemon zest, parsley, and dill or basil. Toss gently to combine.

Step 4: Season and Serve
1. Taste and adjust seasoning with additional salt, pepper, or lemon juice if needed.
2. Serve warm or at room temperature.

Serving Suggestions
- Pair with grilled fish, chicken, or tofu for a complete Mediterranean-inspired meal.
- Serve as a side dish alongside a fresh green salad with a simple vinaigrette.
- Enjoy a light vegetarian lunch with a dollop of hummus on the side.

This **Barley Pilaf with Roasted Vegetables and Fresh Herbs** is a deliciously healthy dish highlighting the Mediterranean Diet's emphasis on whole grains, fresh produce, and vibrant flavors. Its balance of nutrients and comforting texture make it perfect for any meal. Enjoy!

6. Spaghetti Aglio e Olio with Shrimp and Red Pepper Flakes

Yield: 2 servings | **Preparation Time:** 10 minutes | **Cooking Time:** 15 minutes

Ingredients	Nutritional Information (Per Serving)
Base Ingredients • 6 oz whole wheat spaghetti • 2 tbsp extra virgin olive oil • 3 garlic cloves, thinly sliced • 1/2 tsp red pepper flakes (adjust to taste) • 1/2 lb shrimp, peeled and deveined • 1/4 tsp sea salt (or to taste) • 1/8 tsp ground black pepper • 2 tbsp fresh parsley, chopped • 1 tbsp fresh lemon juice • 1/4 cup reserved pasta cooking water **Optional Customizations** • Add 2 tbsp grated Parmesan or Pecorino Romano for a cheesy flavor. • Include 1/4 cup halved cherry tomatoes for extra freshness. • Substitute shrimp with scallops or chicken for variety.	• **Calories:** 360 kcal • **Protein:** 25 g • **Carbohydrates:** 40 g • **Fats:** 10 g • **Fiber:** 7 g • **Cholesterol:** 140 mg • **Sodium:** 320 mg • **Potassium:** 400 mg

Equipment Needed
- Large pot for boiling pasta
- Large skillet
- Tongs

Step-by-Step Instructions
Step 1: Cook the Pasta
1. Bring a large pot of salted water to a boil.
2. Add the whole wheat spaghetti and cook until al dente, following the package instructions (approximately 8–10 minutes).
3. Reserve 1/4 cup of the pasta cooking water, then drain the pasta and set aside.

Step 2: Sauté the Garlic and Shrimp
1. Heat the olive oil in a large skillet over medium heat.
2. Add the garlic and red pepper flakes, cooking for 1–2 minutes until the garlic is fragrant and golden (but not burned).
3. Add the shrimp to the skillet, season with salt and black pepper, and cook for 2–3 minutes per side or until pink and fully cooked.

Step 3: Combine the Pasta and Sauce
1. Reduce the heat to low and add the cooked pasta to the skillet with the shrimp.
2. Pour in the reserved pasta water and toss to combine, ensuring the pasta is evenly coated in the garlic-infused oil.
3. Stir in the fresh parsley and lemon juice, tossing gently to incorporate.

Step 4: Serve
1. Divide the spaghetti between two plates or bowls.
2. Garnish with additional parsley and a sprinkle of red pepper flakes, if desired.

Serving Suggestions
- Serve with a side of arugula salad drizzled with lemon and olive oil.
- Pair with a slice of whole-grain bread for a complete Mediterranean-inspired meal.
- Enjoy with a chilled white wine or sparkling water infused with citrus.

7. Saffron Rice with Toasted Almonds and Golden Raisins

Yield: 2 servings | **Preparation Time**: 10 minutes | **Cooking Time**: 25 minutes

Ingredients	Nutritional Information (Per Serving)
Base Ingredients - 1/2 cup basmati rice - 1 cup low-sodium vegetable or chicken broth - 1/8 tsp saffron threads, soaked in 1 tbsp warm water - 1/4 cup golden raisins - 2 tbsp slivered almonds, toasted - 1 tbsp olive oil or unsalted butter - 1/4 tsp sea salt (or to taste) - 1/8 tsp ground black pepper **Optional Customizations** - Add 1/4 tsp ground cinnamon or cardamom for a warm spice note. - Include 2 tbsp chopped fresh parsley for a fresh, herbal touch. - Substitute basmati rice with long-grain brown rice for extra fiber.	- **Calories:** 220 kcal - **Protein:** 5 g - **Carbohydrates:** 32 g - **Fats:** 8 g - **Fiber:** 2 g - **Cholesterol:** 0 mg (with butter: 10 mg) - **Sodium:** 180 mg - **Potassium:** 230 mg

Equipment Needed
- Medium saucepan with lid
- Small skillet
- Small bowl

Step-by-Step Instructions
Step 1: Prepare the Saffron
1. Place the saffron threads in a small bowl and add 1 tablespoon of warm water. Let it steep while you prepare the other ingredients.

Step 2: Toast the Almonds
1. Heat a small skillet over medium heat.
2. Add the slivered almonds and toast for 2–3 minutes, stirring frequently, until golden and fragrant. Remove from heat and set aside.

Step 3: Cook the Rice
1. heat the olive oil or butter over medium heat in a medium saucepan.
2. Add the rice and sauté for 1–2 minutes until the grains are lightly toasted.
3. Stir in the vegetable or chicken broth, saffron (and soaking water), sea salt, and black pepper.
4. Bring to a boil, then reduce the heat to low, cover, and simmer for 15–18 minutes, or until the rice is tender and the liquid is absorbed.

Step 4: Add Raisins and Finish
1. During the last 5 minutes of cooking, sprinkle the golden raisins over the rice and cover the saucepan. This allows the raisins to soften and plump up.
2. fluff the rice with a fork to mix in the raisins once cooked.

Step 5: Garnish and Serve
1. Transfer the rice to a serving dish and sprinkle the toasted almonds.
2. Garnish with chopped parsley, if using.

Serving Suggestions

- Pair with grilled chicken, lamb, or fish for a Mediterranean-inspired meal.
- Serve as a side dish alongside roasted vegetables or a fresh green salad.
- Enjoy a light vegetarian main course with a dollop of plain Greek yogurt on the side.

This **Saffron Rice with Toasted Almonds and Golden Raisins** is a fragrant and flavorful dish that highlights the richness of Mediterranean ingredients. Its combination of heart-healthy fats, whole grains, and subtle sweetness makes it nutritious and delicious. Enjoy!

1. Grilled Salmon with Dill Yogurt Sauce

Yield: 2 servings | **Preparation Time:** 10 minutes | **Cooking Time:** 10 minutes

Ingredients	Nutritional Information (Per Serving)
For the Salmon • 2 salmon fillets (4–6 oz each) • 1 tbsp extra virgin olive oil • 1 tsp fresh lemon juice • 1/4 tsp sea salt • 1/8 tsp ground black pepper **For the Dill Yogurt Sauce** • 1/2 cup plain Greek yogurt • 1 tbsp fresh dill, finely chopped • 1 tsp fresh lemon juice • 1/2 tsp lemon zest • 1 small garlic clove, minced **Optional Customizations** • Add 1/2 tsp Dijon mustard to the sauce for a tangy twist. • Sprinkle red chili flakes on the salmon for a hint of spice. • Use lime juice and zest instead of lemon for a zesty variation.	• **Calories:** 320 kcal • **Protein:** 34 g • **Carbohydrates:** 2 g • **Fats:** 20 g • **Fiber:** 0 g • **Cholesterol:** 70 mg • **Sodium:** 300 mg • **Potassium:** 600 mg

Equipment Needed
- Grill pan or outdoor grill
- Mixing bowl
- Small whisk

Step-by-Step Instructions
Step 1: Prepare the Salmon
1. Pat the salmon fillets dry with a paper towel.
2. Brush both sides of the salmon with olive oil and drizzle with lemon juice.
3. Season with sea salt and black pepper.

Step 2: Make the Dill Yogurt Sauce
1. In a small mixing bowl, combine the Greek yogurt, dill, lemon juice, lemon zest, minced garlic, sea salt, and black pepper.
2. Mix well and refrigerate until ready to serve.

Step 3: Grill the Salmon
1. Heat a grill pan or outdoor grill over medium-high heat.
2. Place the salmon fillets skin-side down and grill for 4–5 minutes.
3. Flip the fillets and grill for 4–5 minutes until the salmon is cooked and flakes easily with a fork.

Step 4: Plate and Serve
1. Transfer the grilled salmon to plates.
2. Spoon the dill yogurt sauce over the salmon or serve it on the side.

Serving Suggestions
- Serve with steamed asparagus or roasted vegetables for a balanced meal.
- Pair with a Mediterranean quinoa salad or a warm lentil salad.
- Enjoy with a slice of whole-grain bread or a tiny saffron rice.

2. Mediterranean Baked Cod with Lemon and Capers

Yield: 2 servings | **Preparation Time:** 10 minutes | **Cooking Time:** 15–20 minutes

Ingredients	Nutritional Information (Per Serving)
For the Cod	• **Calories:** 210 kcal
• 2 cod fillets (4–6 oz each)	• **Protein:** 30 g
• 1 tbsp extra virgin olive oil	• **Carbohydrates:** 4 g
• 2 tbsp fresh lemon juice	• **Fats:** 8 g
• 1 tsp lemon zest	• **Fiber:** 1 g
• 1 garlic clove, minced	• **Cholesterol:** 70 mg
• 1 tbsp capers, drained	• **Sodium:** 320 mg
• 1/4 cup cherry tomatoes, halved	• **Potassium:** 550 mg
• 2 tbsp fresh parsley, chopped	
• 1/4 tsp sea salt	
• 1/8 tsp ground black pepper	
Optional Customizations	
• Add 1/4 tsp red chili flakes for a touch of heat.	
• Substitute cod with haddock or halibut.	
• Include 1/4 cup sliced Kalamata olives for added Mediterranean flair.	

Equipment Needed
- Baking dish
- Mixing bowl
- Foil or parchment paper (optional for easier cleanup)

Step-by-Step Instructions

Step 1: Preheat the Oven
1. Preheat your oven to 375°F (190°C).

Step 2: Prepare the Cod
1. Pat the cod fillets dry with a paper towel.
2. Place the fillets in a baking dish, ensuring they are not overlapping.

Step 3: Make the Lemon-Caper Mixture
1. In a small mixing bowl, combine olive oil, lemon juice, lemon zest, minced garlic, capers, sea salt, and black pepper.
2. Drizzle the mixture evenly over the cod fillets.

Step 4: Add Vegetables and Herbs
1. Scatter the cherry tomato halves around the cod fillets in the baking dish.
2. Sprinkle the fresh parsley over the top.

Step 5: Bake the Cod
1. Cover the baking dish with foil (optional for steaming effect) and bake for 15–20 minutes until the cod is opaque and flakes easily with a fork.
2. Remove the foil for the last 5 minutes of baking to allow the tomatoes to slightly caramelize.

Serving Suggestions
- Serve with a side of quinoa, couscous, or roasted vegetables.
- Pair with a fresh green salad drizzled with olive oil and lemon juice.
- Enjoy with crusty whole-grain bread to soak up the flavorful juices.

3. Garlic Butter Shrimp with Zucchini Noodles

Yield: 2 servings | **Preparation Time:** 10 minutes | **Cooking Time:** 10 minutes

Ingredients	Nutritional Information (Per Serving)
For the Shrimp • 1/2 lb shrimp, peeled and deveined • 2 tbsp unsalted butter (or olive oil for a dairy-free option) • 2 garlic cloves, minced • 1/4 tsp sea salt • 1/8 tsp ground black pepper • 1/4 tsp red pepper flakes (optional, for spice) • 1 tbsp fresh lemon juice • 1 tbsp fresh parsley, chopped **For the Zucchini Noodles** • 2 medium zucchini, spiralized • 1 tbsp extra virgin olive oil • 1/4 tsp sea salt • 1/8 tsp ground black pepper **Optional Customizations** • Add 1/4 cup halved cherry tomatoes for a burst of color and sweetness. • Sprinkle grated Parmesan or Pecorino Romano on top for extra flavor. • Substitute zucchini noodles with spaghetti squash or whole wheat pasta if desired.	• **Calories:** 220 kcal • **Protein:** 24 g • **Carbohydrates:** 7 g • **Fats:** 12 g • **Fiber:** 2 g • **Cholesterol:** 170 mg • **Sodium:** 320 mg • **Potassium:** 600 mg

Equipment Needed

- Spiralizer or julienne peeler
- Large skillet
- Tongs

Step-by-Step Instructions

Step 1: Prepare the Zucchini Noodles

1. Use a spiralizer or julienne peeler to create zucchini noodles.
2. Heat olive oil in a large skillet over medium heat.
3. Add the zucchini noodles, season with salt and pepper, and sauté for 2–3 minutes until slightly softened.
4. Remove from heat and set aside.

Step 2: Cook the Shrimp

1. In the same skillet, melt the butter over medium heat. (Use olive oil if dairy-free.)
2. Add the minced garlic and cook for 1 minute, stirring constantly, until fragrant.
3. Add the shrimp to the skillet and season with sea salt, black pepper, and red pepper flakes (if using).
4. Cook the shrimp for 2–3 minutes per side or until pink and opaque.
5. Stir in the lemon juice and parsley, tossing to coat the shrimp in the garlic butter sauce.

Step 3: Combine and Serve

1. Add the zucchini noodles back to the skillet with the shrimp.
2. Toss gently to combine and heat through.

Serving Suggestions

- Serve warm as a complete low-carb meal.
- Pair with a simple green salad or steamed asparagus for extra vegetables.
- Enjoy with a slice of whole-grain bread to soak up the garlic butter sauce.

4. Tuna Steak with Olive Tapenade and Fresh Herbs

Yield: 2 servings | **Preparation Time:** 10 minutes | **Cooking Time:** 8 minutes

Ingredients	Nutritional Information (Per Serving)
For the Tuna Steaks • 2 tuna steaks (6 oz each) • 1 tbsp extra virgin olive oil • 1/4 tsp sea salt • 1/8 tsp ground black pepper • 1/2 tsp lemon zest **For the Olive Tapenade** • 1/4 cup Kalamata olives, pitted and finely chopped • 1 tbsp capers, drained and rinsed • 1 small garlic clove, minced • 1 tbsp extra virgin olive oil • 1 tsp fresh lemon juice • 1 tbsp fresh parsley, chopped **Optional Customizations** • Add 1 tsp chopped sun-dried tomatoes to the tapenade for a sweeter flavor. • Include a pinch of red chili flakes for a spicy kick. • Use basil or dill in addition to parsley for extra herbal complexity.	• **Calories:** 290 kcal • **Protein:** 40 g • **Carbohydrates:** 2 g • **Fats:** 14 g • **Fiber:** 1 g • **Cholesterol:** 55 mg • **Sodium:** 320 mg • **Potassium:** 700 mg

Equipment Needed
- Medium skillet or grill pan
- Mixing bowl
- Tongs

Step-by-Step Instructions

Step 1: Prepare the Olive Tapenade
1. In a small mixing bowl, combine the chopped Kalamata olives, capers, minced garlic, olive oil, lemon juice, parsley, and oregano.
2. Mix well and set aside to let the flavors meld.

Step 2: Season the Tuna Steaks
1. Pat the tuna steaks dry with a paper towel.
2. Brush both sides with olive oil and season with sea salt, black pepper, and lemon zest.

Step 3: Cook the Tuna Steaks
1. Heat a skillet or grill pan over medium-high heat.
2. Place the tuna steaks in the hot skillet and sear for 2–3 minutes per side for medium-rare, or adjust the cooking time to your preferred doneness.

Step 4: Assemble the Dish
1. Remove the tuna steaks from the skillet and let them rest for 1 minute.
2. Spoon the olive tapenade generously over each tuna steak.

Serving Suggestions
- Serve with a side of roasted vegetables (e.g., zucchini, eggplant, or bell peppers).
- Pair with a light quinoa salad or couscous for a complete Mediterranean meal.
- Enjoy with a slice of whole-grain bread or pita for soaking up the tapenade.

This **Tuna Steak with Olive Tapenade and Fresh Herbs** is a quick, nutritious, and elegant dish that perfectly captures the essence of Mediterranean cuisine. It's high in omega-3s, heart-healthy fats, and fresh herbs, making it a delightful choice for a healthy and flavorful meal. Enjoy!

5. Seafood Paella with Saffron and Fresh Vegetables

Yield: 2 servings | Preparation Time: 15 minutes | Cooking Time: 30 minutes

Ingredients	Nutritional Information (Per Serving)
Base Ingredients • 1/2 cup Arborio rice or short-grain paella rice • 1 1/2 cups low-sodium chicken or seafood broth • 1/8 tsp saffron threads, steeped in 2 tbsp warm water • 1/4 cup diced onion • 1/2 cup diced red bell pepper • 1/2 cup diced zucchini • 2 garlic cloves, minced • 1/2 cup diced tomatoes • 1 tbsp extra virgin olive oil • 4 large shrimp, peeled and deveined • 4 mussels, scrubbed and de-bearded • 1/4 cup peas (fresh or frozen) • 1/4 tsp smoked paprika • 1/4 tsp sea salt (or to taste) • 1/8 tsp ground black pepper • 1 tbsp fresh parsley, chopped	• **Calories:** 310 kcal • **Protein:** 20 g • **Carbohydrates:** 32 g • **Fats:** 10 g • **Fiber:** 4 g • **Cholesterol:** 120 mg • **Sodium:** 320 mg • **Potassium:** 400 mg

Equipment Needed
- Large skillet or paella pan
- Wooden spoon or spatula

Step-by-Step Instructions

Step 1: Prepare the Saffron Broth
1. Heat the chicken or seafood broth in a small saucepan until warm.
2. Add the saffron threads (with the soaking water) to the broth and let it infuse while you prepare the other ingredients.

Step 2: Sauté the Vegetables
1. Heat the olive oil in a large skillet or paella pan over medium heat.
2. Add the onion, red bell pepper, zucchini, and sauté for 3–4 minutes until softening.
3. Stir in the garlic, diced tomatoes, smoked paprika, salt, and black pepper. Cook for another 1–2 minutes.

Step 3: Cook the Rice
1. Add the rice to the skillet, stirring to coat it with the vegetable mixture.
2. Slowly pour in the saffron-infused broth. Spread the rice evenly across the pan and bring it to a simmer.
3. Reduce the heat to medium-low and let the rice cook, uncovered, for 15–18 minutes without stirring until most of the liquid is absorbed.

Step 4: Add the Seafood
1. Arrange the shrimp and mussels on top of the rice.
2. Scatter the peas over the pan.
3. Cover the skillet with a lid or foil and cook for 5–7 minutes, or until the shrimp are pink and opaque and the mussels have opened (discard any remaining closed).

Step 5: Garnish and Serve
1. Remove the skillet from heat and let the paella rest for 2 minutes.
2. Sprinkle with fresh parsley before serving.

Serving Suggestions
- Pair with a crisp green salad with olive oil and lemon juice.
- Serve with crusty whole-grain bread to soak up the flavorful juices.
- Enjoy with a glass of chilled white wine or sparkling water with lemon.

This **Seafood Paella with Saffron and Fresh Vegetables** captures the vibrant and healthful essence of the Mediterranean Diet. It's a balanced and nutrient-rich dish that brings together the best of seafood, grains, and fresh produce for a meal that's as delicious as it is wholesome. Enjoy!

6. Broiled Sardines with Lemon and Fresh Parsley

Yield: 2 servings | **Preparation Time:** 10 minutes | **Cooking Time:** 8 minutes

Ingredients	Nutritional Information (Per Serving)
Base Ingredients • 8 whole fresh sardines, cleaned and scaled (about 6 oz each) • 2 tbsp extra virgin olive oil • 1/4 tsp sea salt • 1/8 tsp ground black pepper • 1 small lemon, sliced thinly • 1 tbsp fresh lemon juice • 2 tbsp fresh parsley, chopped • 1 garlic clove, minced	• **Calories:** 280 kcal • **Protein:** 30 g • **Carbohydrates:** 1 g • **Fats:** 18 g • **Fiber:** 0 g • **Cholesterol:** 90 mg • **Sodium:** 320 mg • **Potassium:** 450 mg

Optional Customizations	
• Add 1/2 tsp red chili flakes for a spicy kick. • Include 1 tsp fresh thyme or oregano for additional herbal flavor. • Substitute lemon with lime for a zesty twist.	

Equipment Needed
- Baking sheet
- Aluminum foil or parchment paper
- Pastry brush

Step-by-Step Instructions

Step 1: Preheat the Broiler
1. Preheat your oven's broiler to high.
2. Line a baking sheet with aluminum foil or parchment paper for easier cleanup.

Step 2: Prepare the Sardines
1. Pat the sardines dry with a paper towel and place them on the prepared baking sheet.
2. Brush both sides of the sardines with olive oil and season with sea salt and black pepper.
3. Arrange the lemon slices over and around the sardines.

Step 3: Broil the Sardines
1. Place the baking sheet under the broiler, about 4–6 inches from the heat source.
2. Broil for 4 minutes, then flip the sardines carefully and broil for 3–4 minutes, or until the skin is crispy and the fish is cooked.

Step 4: Garnish and Serve
1. Drizzle the sardines with fresh lemon juice and sprinkle with chopped parsley and minced garlic.

Serving Suggestions
- Pair with a light green salad and a side of roasted vegetables.

- Serve alongside a simple quinoa or couscous salad for a complete Mediterranean-inspired meal.
- Enjoy with a slice of crusty whole-grain bread to soak up the flavorful juices.

This **Broiled Sardines with Lemon and Fresh Parsley** recipe is a quick and flavorful way to enjoy the health benefits of Mediterranean seafood. Its combination of healthy fats, lean protein, and fresh herbs makes it a nutrient-rich dish that's as delicious as it is wholesome. Enjoy!

7. Scallops in White Wine and Garlic Sauce

Yield: 2 servings | **Preparation Time:** 10 minutes | **Cooking Time:** 10 minutes

Ingredients	Nutritional Information (Per Serving)
For the Scallops • 12 large sea scallops (about 1 lb), patted dry • 1 tbsp extra virgin olive oil • 1 tbsp unsalted butter (or an extra tbsp olive oil for dairy-free) • 2 garlic cloves, minced • 1/4 cup dry white wine (e.g., Sauvignon Blanc or Pinot Grigio) • 1 tbsp fresh lemon juice • 1/4 tsp sea salt (or to taste) • 1/8 tsp ground black pepper • 1 tbsp fresh parsley, chopped **Optional Customizations** • Add 1/4 tsp red pepper flakes for a spicy kick. • Include 1 tsp capers for extra brininess. • Substitute lemon juice with lime juice for a zesty twist.	• **Calories:** 220 kcal • **Protein:** 25 g • **Carbohydrates:** 3 g • **Fats:** 12 g • **Fiber:** 0 g • **Cholesterol:** 40 mg • **Sodium:** 280 mg • **Potassium:** 400 mg

Equipment Needed

- Large skillet
- Tongs
- Small whisk

Step-by-Step Instructions

Step 1: Prepare the Scallops

- Pat the scallops dry with a paper towel to ensure a good sear.
- Season both sides of the scallops with sea salt and black pepper.

Step 2: Sear the Scallops

- Heat the olive oil and butter in a large skillet over medium-high heat until hot but not smoking.
- Add the scallops to the skillet in a single layer, leaving space between each one.
- Sear for 2–3 minutes on each side until golden brown and cooked through. Remove the scallops from the skillet and set aside.

Step 3: Make the White Wine and Garlic Sauce

- Reduce the heat to medium and add the minced garlic to the skillet. Sauté for 30 seconds, stirring frequently, until fragrant.
- Pour in the white wine and lemon juice, scraping any browned bits from the bottom of the skillet with a wooden spoon.
- Simmer for 2–3 minutes until the sauce slightly reduces.

Step 4: Combine and Serve

- Return the scallops to the skillet and spoon the sauce over them to coat. Heat for 1–2 minutes.
- Sprinkle with fresh parsley before serving.

Serving Suggestions

- Serve over a bed of zucchini noodles, whole-grain pasta, or quinoa for a complete Mediterranean-inspired meal.
- Pair with steamed asparagus or roasted vegetables for a healthy side.
- Enjoy with a slice of whole-grain bread to soak up the flavorful sauce.

This **Scallops in White Wine and Garlic Sauce** recipe is a delightful showcase of Mediterranean flavors. It's packed with protein, healthy fats, and vibrant ingredients, making it a perfect dish for a nutritious and elegant meal. Enjoy!

1. Lemon and Herb Roasted Chicken with Olive Oil

Yield: 2 servings | **Preparation Time:** 15 minutes | **Cooking Time:** 40-45 minutes

Ingredients	Nutritional Information (Per Servin)
Ingredients **Base Ingredients** • 2 bone-in, skin-on chicken thighs or 2 chicken leg quarters • 2 tbsp extra virgin olive oil • 2 tbsp fresh lemon juice • 1 tsp lemon zest • 1 tbsp fresh rosemary, chopped • 1 tbsp fresh thyme leaves • 1 tbsp fresh parsley, chopped (plus more for garnish) • 3 garlic cloves, minced • 1/2 cup chicken broth or white wine **Optional Customizations** • Add 1/4 tsp red pepper flakes for a spicy kick. • Substitute thyme with oregano or marjoram for a flavor variation. • Include 1/4 cup pitted Kalamata olives for an extra Mediterranean touch.	• **Calories:** 330 kcal • **Protein:** 24 g • **Carbohydrates:** 2 g • **Fats:** 25 g • **Fiber:** 0 g • **Cholesterol:** 100 mg • **Sodium:** 280 mg • **Potassium:** 340 mg

Equipment Needed
- Baking dish
- Small mixing bowl
- Oven

Step-by-Step Instructions

Step 1: Preheat the Oven
1. Preheat your oven to 400°F (200°C).

Step 2: Prepare the Marinade
1. In a small mixing bowl, combine the olive oil, lemon juice, lemon zest, rosemary, thyme, parsley, garlic, sea salt, and black pepper. Mix well to create a marinade.

Step 3: Marinate the Chicken
1. Pat the chicken pieces dry with a paper towel.
2. Rub the marinade evenly over the chicken, ensuring the mixture gets under the skin for maximum flavor. Let the chicken rest for 10 minutes while the oven heats.

Step 4: Arrange in the Baking Dish
1. Place the chicken pieces in a baking dish, skin-side up.
2. Pour the chicken broth or white wine around the chicken in the dish.

Step 5: Roast the Chicken
1. When measured with a meat thermometer, Roast the chicken in the oven for 40–45 minutes or until the internal temperature reaches 165°F (74°C).
2. During the last 5–7 minutes of cooking, switch the oven to broil to crisp the skin, if desired.

Step 6: Garnish and Serve
1. Remove the chicken from the oven and let it rest for 5 minutes.
2. Garnish with additional chopped parsley before serving.

Serving Suggestions
- Serve alongside roasted vegetables like zucchini, eggplant, and cherry tomatoes for a complete Mediterranean meal.
- Pair with a simple arugula salad with olive oil and balsamic vinegar.
- Enjoy with a side of quinoa or whole-grain couscous to soak up the flavorful juices.

This **Lemon and Herb Roasted Chicken with Olive Oil** is a delicious and healthy dish that highlights the fresh, vibrant flavors of the Mediterranean Diet. Its balance of lean protein, heart-healthy fats, and aromatic herbs makes it a perfect choice for any meal. Enjoy!

2. Chicken Souvlaki with Tzatziki Sauce

Yield: 2 servings | **Preparation Time:** 20 minutes (plus 30 minutes marinating) | **Cooking Time:** 10–15 minutes

Ingredients	Nutritional Information (Per Serving)
For the Chicken Souvlaki	<ul><li>**Calories:** 280 kcal</li><li>**Protein:** 34 g</li><li>**Carbohydrates:** 5 g</li><li>**Fats:** 14 g</li><li>**Fiber:** 1 g</li><li>**Cholesterol:** 85 mg</li><li>**Sodium:** 300 mg</li><li>**Potassium:** 450 mg</li></ul>
<ul><li>2 boneless, skinless chicken breasts (about 12 oz total), cut into 1-inch cubes</li><li>2 tbsp extra virgin olive oil</li><li>2 tbsp fresh lemon juice</li><li>1 tsp lemon zest</li><li>2 garlic cloves, minced</li><li>1 tsp dried oregano</li><li>1/2 tsp sea salt</li><li>1/4 tsp ground black pepper</li></ul>	

For the Tzatziki Sauce	
<ul><li>1/2 cup plain Greek yogurt</li><li>1/4 cup cucumber, grated and squeezed to remove excess liquid</li><li>1 tsp fresh dill, chopped</li><li>1 small garlic clove, minced</li><li>1 tbsp fresh lemon juice</li><li>1/8 tsp sea salt</li></ul>	

Equipment Needed

- Mixing bowls
- Skewers (soak wooden skewers in water for 30 minutes to prevent burning)
- Grill or grill pan

Step-by-Step Instructions

Step 1: Marinate the Chicken

1. whisk together olive oil, lemon juice, lemon zest, minced garlic, oregano, sea salt, and black pepper in a mixing bowl.
2. Add the chicken cubes to the marinade, tossing to coat evenly.
3. Cover and refrigerate for at least 30 minutes or up to 2 hours for more flavor.

Step 2: Prepare the Tzatziki Sauce

1. In a small bowl, combine Greek yogurt, grated cucumber, dill, minced garlic, lemon juice, and sea salt.
2. Mix well and refrigerate until ready to serve.

Step 3: Assemble the Skewers

1. Thread the marinated chicken pieces onto skewers.

Step 4: Grill the Chicken

1. Preheat a grill or grill pan over medium-high heat.
2. Lightly oil the grill grates to prevent sticking.

3. Place the chicken skewers on the grill and cook for 4–5 minutes per side until the chicken is cooked through and has a nice char (internal temperature of 165°F/74°C).

Step 5: Serve

1. Remove the chicken skewers from the grill and let them rest for 2 minutes.
2. Serve alongside the tzatziki sauce.

Serving Suggestions

- Pair with a Greek salad with cucumbers, tomatoes, red onion, Kalamata olives, and feta.
- Serve with whole-grain pita bread or a side of quinoa for a complete Mediterranean-inspired meal.
- Enjoy with a squeeze of fresh lemon and a garnish of parsley.

This **Chicken Souvlaki with Tzatziki Sauce** is a perfect example of the Mediterranean Diet's emphasis on lean protein, fresh vegetables, and healthy fats. It's a flavorful, satisfying, and nutritious meal that's easy to prepare and delicious. Enjoy!

3. Mediterranean Baked Chicken Thighs with Tomatoes and Olives

Yield: 2 servings | **Preparation Time:** 15 minutes | **Cooking Time:** 35-40 minutes

Ingredients	Nutritional Information (Per Serving)
Base Ingredients - 2 bone-in, skin-on chicken thighs (about 12 oz total) - 1 tbsp extra virgin olive oil - 1 cup cherry tomatoes, halved - 1/4 cup Kalamata olives, pitted and halved - 1/4 cup red onion, thinly sliced - 2 garlic cloves, minced - 1 tsp dried oregano - 1/2 tsp dried thyme (or 1 tsp fresh thyme) - 1/4 tsp sea salt (or to taste) - 1/8 tsp ground black pepper - 1/4 cup low-sodium chicken broth or white wine - 1 tbsp fresh parsley, chopped (for garnish) **Optional Customizations** - Add 1/4 tsp red pepper flakes for a spicy kick. - Include 1 tbsp capers for an extra layer of briny flavor. - Substitute Kalamata olives with green Castelvetrano olives for a milder taste.	- **Calories:** 320 kcal - **Protein:** 22 g - **Carbohydrates:** 6 g - **Fats:** 22 g - **Fiber:** 2 g - **Cholesterol:** 95 mg - **Sodium:** 380 mg - **Potassium:** 450 mg

Equipment Needed
- Baking dish
- Mixing bowl
- Aluminum foil (optional)

Step-by-Step Instructions

Step 1: Preheat the Oven
1. Preheat your oven to 400°F (200°C).

Step 2: Season the Chicken Thighs
1. Pat the chicken thighs dry with a paper towel.
2. Rub the chicken with olive oil and season with sea salt, black pepper, and 1/2 tsp of oregano.

Step 3: Prepare the Tomato-Olive Mixture
1. Mix cherry tomatoes, olives, red onion, garlic, dried thyme, and the remaining oregano in a mixing bowl. Toss well to coat.

Step 4: Assemble the Dish
1. Place the seasoned chicken thighs in a baking dish, skin-side up.
2. Surround the chicken with the tomato-olive mixture.
3. Pour the chicken broth or white wine into the dish.

Step 5: Bake the Chicken
1. Cover the dish with aluminum foil (optional for a softer texture) and bake for 25 minutes.
2. Remove the foil and bake for 10–15 minutes, until the chicken skin is golden and crispy and the internal temperature reaches 165°F (74°C).

Step 6: Garnish and Serve
1. Remove the dish from the oven and let it rest for 5 minutes.
2. Sprinkle with fresh parsley before serving.

Serving Suggestions

- Serve with a side of quinoa, whole-grain couscous, or crusty whole-grain bread to soak up the flavorful juices.
- Pair with a simple green salad with olive oil and balsamic vinegar.
- Enjoy a glass of sparkling water with lemon or your favorite Mediterranean-inspired drink.

4. Grilled Chicken with Artichoke and Spinach Sauce

Yield: 2 servings | **Preparation Time:** 15 minutes | **Cooking Time:** 20 minutes

Ingredients	Nutritional Information (Per Serving)
For the Chicken • 2 boneless, skinless chicken breasts (6 oz each) • 1 tbsp extra virgin olive oil • 1 tbsp fresh lemon juice • 1/2 tsp garlic powder • 1/2 tsp dried oregano • 1/4 tsp sea salt • 1/8 tsp ground black pepper **For the Artichoke and Spinach Sauce** • 1 tbsp extra virgin olive oil • 1 garlic clove, minced • 1 cup baby spinach, chopped • 1/2 cup marinated artichoke hearts, drained and chopped • 1/4 cup plain Greek yogurt • 2 tbsp grated Parmesan cheese • 1/4 tsp sea salt • 1/8 tsp ground black pepper	• **Calories:** 320 kcal • **Protein:** 38 g • **Carbohydrates:** 6 g • **Fats:** 15 g • **Fiber:** 2 g • **Cholesterol:** 90 mg • **Sodium:** 320 mg • **Potassium:** 500 mg

Equipment Needed
- Grill or grill pan
- Medium skillet
- Tongs

Step-by-Step Instructions
Step 1: Marinate the Chicken
1. mix olive oil, lemon juice, garlic powder, oregano, sea salt, and black pepper in a small bowl.
2. Rub the marinade evenly over the chicken breasts. Let them marinate for 10–15 minutes while preparing the sauce.

Step 2: Make the Artichoke and Spinach Sauce
1. Heat 1 tablespoon of olive oil in a medium skillet over medium heat.
2. Add minced garlic and sauté for 30 seconds until fragrant.
3. Stir in the chopped spinach and cook for 1–2 minutes until wilted.
4. Add the chopped artichoke hearts and cook for another 1–2 minutes.
5. Reduce the heat to low and stir in the Greek yogurt, Parmesan cheese, sea salt, and black pepper. Mix until combined and creamy. Remove from heat and set aside.

Step 3: Grill the Chicken
1. Preheat a grill or grill pan over medium-high heat.
2. Lightly oil the grill grates to prevent sticking.
3. Place the chicken breasts on the grill and cook for 4–5 minutes per side or until the internal temperature reaches 165°F (74°C).

Step 4: Plate and Serve
1. Transfer the grilled chicken to plates.
2. Spoon the artichoke and spinach sauce over the chicken.
3. Garnish with additional Parmesan or fresh herbs, if desired.

Serving Suggestions
- Serve with a side of roasted vegetables like zucchini, bell peppers, or asparagus.
- Pair with a small portion of quinoa, brown rice, or whole-grain bread for a complete meal.
- Enjoy with a crisp green salad dressed with olive oil and balsamic vinegar.

This **Grilled Chicken with Artichoke and Spinach Sauce** is a perfect example of Mediterranean cuisine's balance of lean protein, healthy fats, and fresh, flavorful ingredients. It's a delicious and nutritious meal that's sure to impress. Enjoy!

5. Moroccan Chicken Tagine with Apricots and Almonds

Yield: 2 servings | **Preparation Time:** 15 minutes | **Cooking Time:** 1 hour

Ingredients	Nutritional Information (Per Serving)
For the Tagine • 2 bone-in, skin-on chicken thighs (about 12 oz total) • 1 tbsp extra virgin olive oil • 1 small onion, finely chopped • 2 garlic cloves, minced • 1/2 cup chicken broth (low-sodium) • 1/4 cup dried apricots, chopped • 2 tbsp slivered almonds, toasted • 1 small cinnamon stick • 1/2 tsp ground cumin • 1/2 tsp ground coriander • 1/4 tsp ground turmeric • 1/4 tsp ground ginger • 1/4 tsp ground cinnamon • 1/4 tsp sea salt (or to taste) • 1/8 tsp ground black pepper • 1/2 cup canned chickpeas, rinsed and drained • 1 tbsp fresh cilantro or parsley, chopped (for garnish)	• **Calories:** 360 kcal • **Protein:** 24 g • **Carbohydrates:** 18 g • **Fats:** 22 g • **Fiber:** 5 g • **Cholesterol:** 90 mg • **Sodium:** 280 mg • **Potassium:** 420 mg

Equipment Needed
- Tagine or Dutch oven (or a large skillet with a lid)
- Small mixing bowl

Step-by-Step Instructions

Step 1: Season and Brown the Chicken
1. Heat the olive oil in a tagine, Dutch oven, or large skillet over medium heat.
2. Season the chicken thighs with sea salt and black pepper.
3. Add the chicken to the pan, skin-side down, and cook for 4–5 minutes per side until golden brown. Remove the chicken and set aside.

Step 2: Sauté the Onions and Spices
1. In the same pan, add the chopped onion and cook for 3–4 minutes until softened.
2. Stir in the garlic, cumin, coriander, turmeric, ginger, cinnamon, and cinnamon stick. Cook for 1 minute until fragrant.

Step 3: Simmer the Tagine
1. Return the chicken to the pan and pour in the chicken broth.
2. Add the chopped apricots, chickpeas, and a pinch of sea salt.
3. Cover the pan and reduce the heat to low. Simmer for 40–45 minutes, stirring occasionally, until the chicken is tender and cooked.

Step 4: Add Almonds and Finish
1. Toast the slivered almonds in a dry skillet over medium heat until golden, about 2–3 minutes.
2. Sprinkle the toasted almonds over the chicken and garnish with fresh cilantro or parsley.

Serving Suggestions
- Serve with whole-grain couscous or quinoa to soak up the flavorful sauce.
- Pair with a simple green salad with olive oil and lemon juice.
- Enjoy with crusty whole-grain bread for a hearty meal.

This **Moroccan Chicken Tagine with Apricots and Almonds** is a beautiful example of the Mediterranean Diet's focus on fresh ingredients, healthy fats, and bold spices. It's a warm and comforting dish perfect for any occasion. Enjoy!

6. Garlic and Paprika Chicken Skewers with Yogurt Marinade

Yield: 2 servings | **Preparation Time:** 20 minutes (plus 30 minutes marinating | **Cooking Time:** 10-12 minutes

Ingredients	Nutritional Information (Per Serving)
For the Chicken Skewers <ul><li>2 boneless, skinless chicken breasts (about 12 oz total), cut into 1-inch cubes</li><li>1/2 cup plain Greek yogurt</li><li>2 tbsp extra virgin olive oil</li><li>2 garlic cloves, minced</li><li>1 tsp smoked paprika</li><li>1 tsp sweet paprika</li><li>1/2 tsp ground cumin</li><li>1/4 tsp sea salt (or to taste)</li><li>1/8 tsp ground black pepper</li><li>1 tbsp fresh lemon juice</li><li>1 tbsp fresh parsley, chopped (for garnish)</li></ul>	<ul><li>**Calories:** 280 kcal</li><li>**Protein:** 38 g</li><li>**Carbohydrates:** 3 g</li><li>**Fats:** 12 g</li><li>**Fiber:** 1 g</li><li>**Cholesterol:** 90 mg</li><li>**Sodium:** 280 mg</li><li>**Potassium:** 450 mg</li></ul>

Equipment Needed

- Skewers (soak wooden skewers in water for 30 minutes to prevent burning)
- Grill or grill pan
- Mixing bowl

Step-by-Step Instructions

Step 1: Prepare the Marinade

1. In a mixing bowl, combine Greek yogurt, olive oil, minced garlic, smoked paprika, sweet paprika, ground cumin, sea salt, black pepper, and lemon juice. Mix well.

Step 2: Marinate the Chicken

1. Add the chicken cubes to the marinade, tossing to coat evenly.
2. Cover and refrigerate for at least 30 minutes or up to 2 hours for maximum flavor.

Step 3: Assemble the Skewers

1. Thread the marinated chicken pieces onto skewers, leaving a little space between each piece for even cooking.

Step 4: Grill the Skewers

1. Preheat a grill or grill pan over medium-high heat.
2. Lightly oil the grill grates to prevent sticking.
3. Place the skewers on the grill and cook for 5–6 minutes per side until the chicken is cooked through and has a light char (internal temperature of 165°F/74°C).

Step 5: Garnish and Serve

1. Transfer the skewers to a serving platter.
2. Garnish with chopped parsley before serving.

Serving Suggestions

- Serve alongside a refreshing cucumber and tomato salad drizzled with olive oil and lemon juice.
- Pair with whole-grain pita bread and a dollop of tzatziki sauce.
- Enjoy with roasted vegetables or a simple quinoa pilaf for a complete Mediterranean-inspired meal.

This **Garlic and Paprika Chicken Skewers with Yogurt Marinade** recipe is a delicious and healthy way to enjoy the bold flavors of the Mediterranean Diet. It's high in protein, low in carbs, and packed with vibrant spices and herbs. Enjoy!

7. Braised Chicken with Lemon, Garlic, and Fresh Thyme

Yield: 2 servings | **Preparation Time:** 15 minutes | **Cooking Time:** 40 minutes

Ingredients	Nutritional Information (Per Serving)
Base Ingredients • 2 bone-in, skin-on chicken thighs (about 12 oz total) • 1 tbsp extra virgin olive oil • 4 garlic cloves, minced • 1/2 cup chicken broth (low-sodium) • 1/4 cup dry white wine (optional, or substitute with more chicken broth) • 1 tbsp fresh lemon juice • 1 tsp lemon zest • 1 tbsp fresh thyme leaves (or 1/2 tsp dried thyme) • 1/4 tsp sea salt (or to taste) • 1/8 tsp ground black pepper • 1 tbsp fresh parsley, chopped (for garnish)	• **Calories:** 280 kcal • **Protein:** 22 g • **Carbohydrates:** 3 g • **Fats:** 20 g • **Fiber:** 1 g • **Cholesterol:** 80 mg • **Sodium:** 270 mg • **Potassium:** 380 mg

Equipment Needed
- Large skillet with lid
- Wooden spoon or spatula

Step-by-Step Instructions
Step 1: Season and Sear the Chicken
1. Pat the chicken thighs dry with a paper towel and season with sea salt and black pepper.
2. Heat the olive oil in a large skillet over medium-high heat.
3. Place the chicken thighs skin-side down and sear for 4–5 minutes until golden brown. Flip and sear the other side for 3 minutes. Remove the chicken and set aside.

Step 2: Sauté the Garlic
1. Reduce the heat to medium and add the minced garlic to the skillet.
2. Sauté for 1 minute, stirring frequently, until fragrant but not browned.

Step 3: Deglaze the Pan
1. Pour in the white wine (if using) and scrape the bottom of the skillet with a wooden spoon to release any browned bits.
2. Add the chicken broth, lemon juice, and lemon zest. Stir to combine.

Step 4: Braise the Chicken
1. Return the chicken thighs to the skillet, skin-side up.
2. Sprinkle the fresh thyme leaves over the chicken.
3. Cover the skillet with a lid, reduce the heat to low, and simmer for 30 minutes or until the chicken is tender and cooked through (internal temperature of 165°F/74°C).

Step 5: Garnish and Serve
1. Remove the chicken from the skillet and spoon the sauce over the top.
2. Garnish with fresh parsley before serving.

Serving Suggestions
- Pair with a side of whole-grain couscous or quinoa to soak up the flavorful sauce.
- Serve alongside steamed asparagus or roasted vegetables for a balanced meal.
- Enjoy with a slice of crusty whole-grain bread for a rustic Mediterranean touch.

This **Braised Chicken with Lemon, Garlic, and Fresh Thyme** recipe captures the essence of the Mediterranean Diet. It combines lean protein, fresh herbs, and heart-healthy olive oil in a simple yet elegant dish. It's perfect for any meal and a delightful way to eat healthy. Enjoy!

1. Lamb Kofta with Mint Yogurt Dip

Yield: 2 servings | **Preparation Time:** 15 minutes | **Cooking Time:** 10-12 minutes

Ingredients	Nutritional Information (Per Serving)
For the Lamb Kofta • 1/2 lb ground lamb • 1 small onion, finely grated • 1 garlic clove, minced • 1 tbsp fresh parsley, finely chopped • 1 tbsp fresh mint, finely chopped • 1 tsp ground cumin • 1 tsp ground coriander • 1/2 tsp smoked paprika • 1/4 tsp ground cinnamon **For the Mint Yogurt Dip** • 1/2 cup plain Greek yogurt • 1 tbsp fresh mint, finely chopped • 1 tsp fresh lemon juice • 1/2 tsp lemon zest • 1 small garlic clove, minced • 1/4 tsp sea salt	• **Calories:** 300 kcal • **Protein:** 28 g • **Carbohydrates:** 6 g • **Fats:** 18 g • **Fiber:** 1 g • **Cholesterol:** 75 mg • **Sodium:** 320 mg • **Potassium:** 400 mg

Equipment Needed
- Large mixing bowl
- Skewers (if using wooden skewers, soak them in water for 30 minutes to prevent burning)
- Grill, grill pan, or broiler

Step-by-Step Instructions

Step 1: Prepare the Mint Yogurt Dip
1. In a small bowl, combine Greek yogurt, mint, lemon juice, lemon zest, garlic, and sea salt.
2. Mix well and refrigerate until ready to serve.

Step 2: Prepare the Lamb Kofta Mixture
1. combine ground lamb, grated onion, minced garlic, parsley, mint, cumin, coriander, paprika, cinnamon, sea salt, and black pepper in a large mixing bowl.
2. Mix well with your hands or a spoon until the ingredients are fully incorporated.

Step 3: Shape the Kofta
1. Divide the lamb mixture into 4 equal portions and shape each portion into an oval or sausage shape around a skewer.
2. If not using skewers, shape the mixture into small patties.

Step 4: Cook the Kofta
1. Preheat a grill, pan, or broiler over medium-high heat.
2. Lightly oil the grates or pan to prevent sticking.
3. Cook the kofta for 3–4 minutes per side or until browned and cooked through (internal temperature of 160°F/71°C).

Step 5: Serve
1. Arrange the lamb kofta on a serving plate.
2. Serve alongside the mint yogurt dip.

Serving Suggestions
- Pair with a simple cucumber and tomato salad drizzled with olive oil and lemon juice.
- Serve with warm whole-grain pita bread or a side of roasted vegetables.
- Add a small portion of quinoa or couscous to complete the meal.

This **Lamb Kofta with Mint Yogurt Dip** is a flavorful and nutritious dish that showcases the Mediterranean Diet's focus on lean protein, fresh herbs, and heart-healthy ingredients. Enjoy this easy-to-make recipe for a delicious and healthy dining experience!

2. Slow-Cooked Beef Stew with Red Wine and Rosemary

Yield: 2 servings | **Preparation Time:** 20 minutes | **Cooking Time:** 2.5–3 hours

Ingredients	Nutritional Information (Per Serving)
Base Ingredients • 8 oz beef stew meat, cut into 1-inch cubes • 1 tbsp extra virgin olive oil • 1 small onion, diced • 2 garlic cloves, minced • 1 small carrot, peeled and sliced • 1 stalk celery, sliced • 1 cup diced tomatoes (canned or fresh) • 1/2 cup red wine (dry, such as Cabernet Sauvignon) • 1/2 cup low-sodium beef broth • 1 small bay leaf • 2 sprigs fresh rosemary (or 1 tsp dried rosemary) • 1/4 tsp sea salt (or to taste) • 1/8 tsp ground black pepper **Optional Customizations** • Add 1 small potato or 1/2 cup butternut squash for a starchy component. • Substitute red wine with additional beef broth if preferred. • Include 1/2 cup chopped mushrooms for added umami flavor.	• **Calories:** 320 kcal • **Protein:** 28 g • **Carbohydrates:** 10 g • **Fats:** 15 g • **Fiber:** 3 g • **Cholesterol:** 80 mg • **Sodium:** 320 mg • **Potassium:** 500 mg

Equipment Needed
- Large skillet or Dutch oven
- Slow cooker (optional for convenience)

Step-by-Step Instructions
Step 1: Sear the Beef
1. Heat olive oil in a large skillet or Dutch oven over medium-high heat.
2. Season the beef cubes with sea salt and black pepper.
3. Sear the beef on all sides until browned, about 4–5 minutes. Remove the beef and set aside.

Step 2: Sauté the Vegetables
1. add the diced onion, carrot, and celery in the same skillet.
2. Sauté for 3–4 minutes until softened, then add the minced garlic and cook for 1 more minute.

Step 3: Deglaze the Pan
1. Pour in the red wine and stir, scraping up any browned bits from the bottom of the skillet.
2. Simmer for 2–3 minutes to reduce slightly.

Step 4: Combine Ingredients and Simmer
1. Add the seared beef to the skillet or transfer everything to a slow cooker.
2. Stir in the diced tomatoes, beef broth, bay leaf, and rosemary sprigs.
3. Cover and simmer on low heat for 2.5–3 hours, stirring occasionally, until the beef is tender and the sauce has thickened.
   - **For a slow cooker:** Cook on low for 6–8 hours or high for 3–4 hours.

Step 5: Garnish and Serve
1. Remove the bay leaf and rosemary sprigs before serving.
2. Garnish with chopped parsley if desired.

Serving Suggestions
- Serve over a bed of whole-grain couscous, quinoa, or mashed cauliflower.
- Pair with a simple green salad with olive oil and balsamic vinegar.
- Enjoy with a slice of crusty whole-grain bread to soak up the rich sauce.

3. Grilled Lamb Chops with Lemon and Oregano

Yield: 2 servings | **Preparation Time:** 15 minutes (plus 30 minutes marinating) | **Cooking Time:** 10-12 minutes

Ingredients	Nutritional Information (Per Serving)
For the Lamb Chops • 4 small lamb loin chops (about 1-inch thick, 5 oz each) • 2 tbsp extra virgin olive oil • 1 tbsp fresh lemon juice • 1 tsp lemon zest • 2 garlic cloves, minced • 1 tsp dried oregano (or 1 tbsp fresh oregano, chopped) • 1/2 tsp sea salt • 1/4 tsp ground black pepper	• **Calories:** 340 kcal • **Protein:** 30 g • **Carbohydrates:** 1 g • **Fats:** 23 g • **Fiber:** 0 g • **Cholesterol:** 90 mg • **Sodium:** 280 mg • **Potassium:** 380 mg

Equipment Needed
- Mixing bowl
- Grill or grill pan
- Tongs

Step-by-Step Instructions
Step 1: Prepare the Marinade
1. whisk together olive oil, lemon juice, lemon zest, minced garlic, oregano, sea salt, and black pepper in a mixing bowl.
2. Place the lamb chops in a shallow dish or zip-top bag and pour the marinade over them.
3. Turn the lamb chops to coat evenly, then cover or seal and refrigerate for at least 30 minutes (or up to 2 hours for deeper flavor).

Step 2: Preheat the Grill
1. Preheat a grill or grill pan over medium-high heat.
2. Lightly oil the grates or grill pan to prevent sticking.

Step 3: Grill the Lamb Chops
1. Remove the lamb chops from the marinade and let any excess drip off.
2. Place the lamb chops on the hot grill and cook for 4–5 minutes per side for medium-rare, or adjust the cooking time to your preferred doneness (internal temperature of 145°F for medium-rare).

Step 4: Rest and Garnish
1. Remove the lamb chops from the grill and let them rest for 5 minutes to allow the juices to redistribute.
2. Garnish with additional lemon zest and fresh oregano, if desired.

Serving Suggestions

- Pair with roasted vegetables such as zucchini, bell peppers, and cherry tomatoes.
- Serve with a simple Greek salad featuring cucumbers, tomatoes, olives, and feta.
- Enjoy with a small portion of whole-grain couscous or quinoa for a complete Mediterranean-inspired meal.

This **Grilled Lamb Chops with Lemon and Oregano** recipe combines the best Mediterranean ingredients to create a delicious and nutritious meal. The bright lemon and earthy oregano enhance the lamb's natural flavors, making it a dish to savor and enjoy. Bon appétit!

4. Ground Beef and Eggplant Moussaka

Yield: 2 servings | **Preparation Time:** 20 minutes | **Cooking Time:** 45 minutes

Ingredients	Nutritional Information (Per Serving)
For the Eggplant Layer • 1 medium eggplant, sliced into 1/4-inch rounds • 1 tbsp extra virgin olive oil • 1/4 tsp sea salt • 1/8 tsp ground black pepper **For the Ground Beef Layer** • 1/2 lb lean ground beef • 1 small onion, finely diced • 2 garlic cloves, minced • 1/2 cup canned diced tomatoes (no salt added) • 1 tbsp tomato paste • 1/2 tsp ground cinnamon • 1/2 tsp dried oregano • 1/4 tsp ground allspice (optional) • 1/4 tsp sea salt (or to taste) • 1/8 tsp ground black pepper **For the Yogurt Topping** • 1/2 cup plain Greek yogurt • 1 egg, lightly beaten • 2 tbsp grated Parmesan cheese • 1/4 tsp ground nutmeg (optional)	• **Calories:** 350 kcal • **Protein:** 28 g • **Carbohydrates:** 15 g • **Fats:** 20 g • **Fiber:** 5 g • **Cholesterol:** 110 mg • **Sodium:** 320 mg • **Potassium:** 600 mg

Equipment Needed
- Large skillet
- Baking dish (8x8 inch or similar size)
- Whisk

Step-by-Step Instructions

Step 1: Prepare the Eggplant
1. Preheat the oven to 400°F (200°C).
2. Arrange the eggplant slices on a baking sheet and brush both sides with olive oil.
3. Season with sea salt and black pepper.
4. Roast in the oven for 15–20 minutes, flipping halfway, until tender and lightly browned.

Step 2: Cook the Ground Beef
1. Heat a skillet over medium heat and add the ground beef. Cook, breaking up the meat, until browned, about 5 minutes.
2. Add the diced onion and garlic, cooking for 2–3 minutes until softened.
3. Stir in the diced tomatoes, tomato paste, cinnamon, oregano, allspice (if using), sea salt, and black pepper.
4. Simmer for 10 minutes, allowing the flavors to meld and the mixture to thicken slightly.

Step 3: Make the Yogurt Topping
1. In a bowl, whisk together the Greek yogurt, beaten egg, Parmesan cheese, and nutmeg (if using).

Step 4: Assemble the Moussaka
1. Lightly grease a baking dish and layer half the roasted eggplant slices on the bottom.
2. Spread the ground beef mixture evenly over the eggplant.
3. Layer the remaining eggplant slices on top of the beef.
4. Pour the yogurt topping over the final eggplant layer, spreading evenly.

Step 5: Bake
1. Reduce the oven temperature to 375°F (190°C).
2. Bake the moussaka for 25–30 minutes or until the topping is golden and set.

Step 6: Rest and Serve
1. Allow the moussaka to rest for 5 minutes before slicing.
2. Garnish with fresh parsley or mint, if desired.

Serving Suggestions
- Pair with a fresh Greek salad with cucumbers, tomatoes, red onion, and feta cheese.
- Serve alongside a whole-grain pita or a small portion of quinoa for added texture.
- Enjoy with steamed green beans or roasted zucchini for extra vegetables.

This **Ground Beef and Eggplant Moussaka** is a healthy and flavorful dish that brings the essence of the Mediterranean Diet to your table. It's a satisfying and nourishing meal with its layers of wholesome ingredients and bold spices. Enjoy!

5. Beef Meatballs in a Spiced Tomato Sauce

Yield: 2 servings | **Preparation Time:** 20 minutes | **Cooking Time:** 30 minutes

Ingredients	Nutritional Information (Per Serving)
For the Meatballs	• **Calories:** 320 kcal
• 1/2 lb lean ground beef	• **Protein:** 28 g
• 2 tbsp finely chopped onion	• **Carbohydrates:** 12 g
• 1 garlic clove, minced	• **Fats:** 18 g
• 1 tbsp fresh parsley, chopped	• **Fiber:** 3 g
• 1 tsp dried oregano	• **Cholesterol:** 85 mg
• 1/2 tsp ground cumin	• **Sodium:** 320 mg
• 1/4 tsp smoked paprika	• **Potassium:** 500 mg
• 1/4 tsp sea salt	
• 1/8 tsp ground black pepper	
• 2 tbsp breadcrumbs (whole wheat if possible)	
• 1 egg, lightly beaten	
For the Spiced Tomato Sauce	
• 1 tbsp extra virgin olive oil	
• 1 small onion, finely chopped	
• 2 garlic cloves, minced	
• 1/2 tsp ground cinnamon	
• 1/2 tsp ground cumin	
• 1/4 tsp red pepper flakes (optional)	
• 1 cup canned crushed tomatoes (no salt added)	
• 1/4 cup low-sodium chicken or vegetable broth	
• 1 tsp dried oregano	
• 1/2 tsp sea salt (or to taste)	
• 1/8 tsp ground black pepper	
• 1 tbsp fresh parsley, chopped (for garnish)	

Equipment Needed
- Large skillet or saucepan
- Mixing bowl
- Wooden spoon

Step-by-Step Instructions

Step 1: Prepare the Meatballs
1. combine ground beef, onion, garlic, parsley, oregano, cumin, smoked paprika, sea salt, black pepper, breadcrumbs, and egg in a mixing bowl.
2. Mix gently with your hands until just combined. Avoid overmixing to keep the meatballs tender.
3. Form the mixture into small meatballs (about 1 inch in diameter).

Step 2: Sear the Meatballs
1. Heat 1/2 tbsp of olive oil in a large skillet over medium heat.
2. Add the meatballs in batches, ensuring they are not overcrowded.
3. Sear the meatballs for 2–3 minutes per side until browned. Remove and set aside.

Step 3: Prepare the Spiced Tomato Sauce
1. heat the remaining 1/2 tbsp olive oil in the same skillet.
2. Add the onion and sauté for 3–4 minutes until softened.
3. Stir in the garlic, cinnamon, cumin, and red pepper flakes (if using). Cook for 1 minute until fragrant.
4. Add the crushed tomatoes, chicken broth, oregano, sea salt, and black pepper. Stir well and bring to a simmer.

Step 4: Simmer the Meatballs
1. Gently add the seared meatballs to the simmering tomato sauce.
2. Cover and cook over low heat for 15–20 minutes, turning the meatballs occasionally to coat them in the sauce.

Step 5: Garnish and Serve
1. Remove the skillet from heat and garnish with fresh parsley.

Serving Suggestions
- Pair with whole-grain couscous, quinoa, or brown rice.
- Serve alongside roasted vegetables or a fresh green salad for a balanced meal.
- Enjoy with a slice of crusty whole-grain bread to soak up the flavorful sauce.

6. Rosemary and Garlic Pork Tenderloin with Pan Jus

Yield: 2 servings | Preparation Time: 15 minutes | Chilling Time: 25–30 minutes

Ingredients	Nutritional Information (Per Serving)
For the Pork Tenderloin • 1 pork tenderloin (about 12 oz) • 2 tbsp extra virgin olive oil, divided • 2 garlic cloves, minced • 1 tsp fresh rosemary, finely chopped (or 1/2 tsp dried rosemary) • 1/2 tsp dried oregano **For the Pan Jus** • 1/4 cup low-sodium chicken broth • 1/4 cup dry white wine (or substitute with more chicken broth) • 1 tsp fresh lemon juice • 1 tsp Dijon mustard • 1 tbsp fresh parsley, chopped (for garnish)	• **Calories:** 280 kcal • **Protein:** 29 g • **Carbohydrates:** 2 g • **Fats:** 16 g • **Fiber:** 0 g • **Cholesterol:** 75 mg • **Sodium:** 220 mg • **Potassium:** 350 mg

Equipment Needed
- Large oven-safe skillet
- Tongs
- Whisk

Step-by-Step Instructions
Step 1: Prepare the Pork Tenderloin
1. Preheat the oven to 400°F (200°C).
2. Pat the pork tenderloin dry with a paper towel.
3. In a small bowl, mix 1 tbsp olive oil, minced garlic, rosemary, oregano, sea salt, and black pepper.
4. Rub the mixture evenly over the pork tenderloin.

Step 2: Sear the Pork
1. Heat the remaining 1 tbsp olive oil in an oven-safe skillet over medium-high heat.
2. Add the pork tenderloin and sear for 2–3 minutes per side until golden brown.

Step 3: Roast the Pork
1. Transfer the skillet to the preheated oven.
2. Roast for 15–20 minutes or until the internal temperature of the pork reaches 145°F (63°C).

Step 4: Rest the Pork and Make the Jus
1. Remove the pork from the skillet and transfer to a plate. Tent with foil and let it rest for 5 minutes.
2. Place the skillet back on the stovetop over medium heat.
3. Add chicken broth and white wine to the skillet, scraping up any browned bits with a wooden spoon.
4. Stir in lemon juice and Dijon mustard, whisking until the jus is slightly thickened (about 2–3 minutes).

Step 5: Slice and Serve
1. Slice the rested pork tenderloin into medallions.
2. Drizzle the pan jus over the pork and garnish with fresh parsley.

Serving Suggestions
- Pair with roasted vegetables such as zucchini, bell peppers, or asparagus.
- Serve alongside a small portion of quinoa, couscous, or mashed cauliflower.
- Enjoy with a crisp green salad dressed with olive oil and balsamic vinegar.

This **Rosemary and Garlic Pork Tenderloin with Pan Jus** perfectly represents the Mediterranean Diet's emphasis on fresh herbs, healthy fats, and lean protein. Its simple preparation and bold flavors make it a delightful dish to savor. Enjoy!

7. Stuffed Bell Peppers with Ground Turkey and Rice

Yield: 2 servings | **Preparation Time:** 15 minutes | **Cooking Time:** 45 minutes

Ingredients	Nutritional Information (Per Serving)
For the Stuffed Peppers • 2 large bell peppers (any color), tops cut off and seeds removed • 1/2 lb lean ground turkey • 1/2 cup cooked brown rice (or quinoa for a gluten-free option) • 1/2 small onion, finely chopped • 1 garlic clove, minced • 1/4 cup canned diced tomatoes (no salt added) • 1 tbsp tomato paste • 1 tsp dried oregano • 1/2 tsp ground cumin • 1/4 tsp smoked paprika • 1/4 tsp sea salt • 1/8 tsp ground black pepper • 1 tbsp fresh parsley, chopped (plus more for garnish) • 1 tbsp extra virgin olive oil **For the Sauce (Optional)** • 1/2 cup tomato sauce • 1/4 cup low-sodium chicken or vegetable broth • 1/2 tsp dried oregano • 1/4 tsp garlic powder	• **Calories:** 280 kcal • **Protein:** 28 g • **Carbohydrates:** 22 g • **Fats:** 10 g • **Fiber:** 4 g • **Cholesterol:** 65 mg • **Sodium:** 350 mg • **Potassium:** 450 mg

Equipment Needed
- Medium skillet
- Baking dish
- Aluminum foil

Step-by-Step Instructions

Step 1: Preheat the Oven
1. Preheat your oven to 375°F (190°C).

Step 2: Prepare the Filling
1. Heat olive oil in a medium skillet over medium heat.
2. Add the onion and garlic, cooking for 2–3 minutes until softened.
3. Stir in the ground turkey, breaking it up with a spoon, and cook until browned, about 5 minutes.
4. Add the diced tomatoes, tomato paste, cooked rice, oregano, cumin, paprika, sea salt, and black pepper. Stir well to combine and cook for an additional 2–3 minutes.
5. Remove from heat and stir in the chopped parsley.

Step 3: Stuff the Peppers
1. Stand the bell peppers upright in a baking dish.
2. Spoon the turkey and rice mixture evenly into each pepper, pressing gently to pack the filling.

Step 4: Prepare the Sauce (Optional)
1. mix the tomato sauce, chicken broth, oregano, and garlic powder in a small bowl.
2. Pour the sauce into the baking dish around the stuffed peppers.

Step 5: Bake
1. Cover the dish with aluminum foil and bake for 30 minutes.
2. Remove the foil and bake for 10–15 minutes or until the peppers are tender and slightly browned on top.

Step 6: Serve
1. Remove the stuffed peppers from the oven and let them rest for 5 minutes.
2. Garnish with additional fresh parsley before serving.

Serving Suggestions
- Pair with steamed green beans or a simple cucumber and tomato salad.
- Serve with whole-grain pita bread for a hearty meal.
- Enjoy with a dollop of Greek yogurt for added creaminess.

This **Stuffed Bell Peppers with Ground Turkey and Rice** recipe combines the rich flavors of Mediterranean spices with wholesome ingredients, making it a healthy and satisfying dish for any occasion. Enjoy!

Chapter 8. Vegetable Recipes

1. Ratatouille with Fresh Herbs and Olive Oil

Yield: 2 servings | **Preparation Time:** 15 minutes | **Cooking Time:** 35–40 minutes

Ingredients	Nutritional Information (Per Serving)
Base Ingredients <ul><li>1 small eggplant, diced into 1-inch cubes</li><li>1 small zucchini, diced into 1-inch cubes</li><li>1 small yellow squash, diced into 1-inch cubes</li><li>1 red bell pepper, diced</li><li>1 small onion, finely chopped</li><li>2 garlic cloves, minced</li><li>1 cup canned diced tomatoes (no salt added)</li><li>2 tbsp extra virgin olive oil</li><li>1 tsp fresh thyme leaves (or 1/2 tsp dried thyme)</li><li>1 tsp fresh rosemary, finely chopped (or 1/2 tsp dried rosemary)</li><li>2 tbsp fresh basil, chopped (plus more for garnish)</li><li>1/4 tsp sea salt (or to taste)</li><li>1/8 tsp ground black pepper</li></ul>	<ul><li>**Calories:** 180 kcal</li><li>**Protein:** 3 g</li><li>**Carbohydrates:** 17 g</li><li>**Fats:** 12 g</li><li>**Fiber:** 6 g</li><li>**Cholesterol:** 0 mg</li><li>**Sodium:** 200 mg</li><li>**Potassium:** 550 mg</li></ul>

Equipment Needed
- Large skillet or sauté pan
- Wooden spoon
- Cutting board and knife

Step-by-Step Instructions
Step 1: Prepare the Vegetables
1. Wash and dice the eggplant, zucchini, yellow squash, and bell pepper into 1-inch cubes.
2. Finely chop the onion and mince the garlic.

Step 2: Sauté the Vegetables
1. Heat 1 tbsp of olive oil in a large skillet over medium heat.
2. Add the eggplant and sauté for 5 minutes, stirring occasionally, until softened. Remove from the skillet and set aside.
3. Add the remaining 1 tbsp olive oil to the skillet. Add the onion, garlic, zucchini, yellow squash, and bell pepper. Sauté for 5–7 minutes until slightly softened.

Step 3: Combine and Simmer
1. Return the eggplant to the skillet and add the canned diced tomatoes, thyme, rosemary, sea salt, and black pepper.
2. Stir well, reduce the heat to low, and cover the skillet.
3. Simmer for 20–25 minutes, stirring occasionally, until the vegetables are tender and the flavors meld together.

Step 4: Add Fresh Herbs and Serve
1. Remove the skillet from heat and stir in the fresh basil.
2. Garnish with additional basil leaves before serving.

Serving Suggestions
- Serve as a main dish with a slice of crusty whole-grain bread or a side of quinoa.
- Pair as a side dish with grilled chicken, fish, or lamb for a hearty Mediterranean meal.
- Enjoy cold or at room temperature as a light salad.

2. Roasted Cauliflower with Lemon and Tahini Drizzle

Yield: 2 servings | **Preparation Time:** 10 minutes | **Cooking Time:** 25–30 minutes

Ingredients	Nutritional Information (Per Serving)
For the Roasted Cauliflower • 1 small head of cauliflower, cut into florets (about 3 cups) • 2 tbsp extra virgin olive oil • 1/2 tsp ground cumin • 1/4 tsp smoked paprika • 1/4 tsp sea salt (or to taste) • 1/8 tsp ground black pepper **For the Tahini Drizzle** • 2 tbsp tahini • 1 tbsp fresh lemon juice • 1 tsp olive oil • 1 small garlic clove, minced • 2–3 tbsp water (to adjust consistency) • Pinch of sea salt	• **Calories:** 180 kcal • **Protein:** 4 g • **Carbohydrates:** 12 g • **Fats:** 14 g • **Fiber:** 4 g • **Cholesterol:** 0 mg • **Sodium:** 200 mg • **Potassium:** 400 mg

Equipment Needed
- Baking sheet
- Mixing bowl
- Small whisk or spoon

Step-by-Step Instructions
Step 1: Preheat the Oven
1. Preheat your oven to 425°F (220°C).

Step 2: Prepare the Cauliflower
1. In a mixing bowl, toss the cauliflower florets with olive oil, cumin, smoked paprika, sea salt, and black pepper.
2. Spread the cauliflower in a single layer on a baking sheet lined with parchment paper.

Step 3: Roast the Cauliflower
1. Roast in the preheated oven for 25–30 minutes, stirring halfway through, until the cauliflower is golden and tender with crispy edges.

Step 4: Make the Tahini Drizzle
1. whisk together tahini, lemon juice, olive oil, minced garlic, and sea salt in a small bowl.
2. Gradually add water, one tablespoon at a time, whisking until the sauce reaches a drizzle-able consistency.

Step 5: Serve
1. Transfer the roasted cauliflower to a serving plate.
2. Drizzle the tahini sauce over the cauliflower.
3. Garnish with fresh herbs or pomegranate seeds, if desired.

Serving Suggestions

- Serve as a side dish with grilled chicken, lamb, or fish.
- Pair with quinoa or couscous for a vegetarian meal.
- Enjoy as an appetizer or snack with warm whole-grain pita bread.

This **Roasted Cauliflower with Lemon and Tahini Drizzle** is a simple yet flavorful way to incorporate vegetables into your diet while embracing the essence of Mediterranean cuisine. Packed with nutrients and bold flavors, it's a dish you'll return to again and again. Enjoy!

3. Eggplant Caponata with Capers and Pine Nuts

Yield: 2 servings | **Preparation Time:** 15 minutes | **Cooking Time:** 25 minutes

Ingredients	Nutritional Information (Per Serving)
Base Ingredients • 1 medium eggplant, diced into 1/2-inch cubes • 2 tbsp extra virgin olive oil • 1/2 small onion, finely chopped • 1 small celery stalk, finely chopped • 1 garlic clove, minced • 1 cup canned diced tomatoes (no salt added) • 1 tbsp red wine vinegar • 1 tbsp capers, rinsed and drained • 2 tbsp pine nuts, toasted • 1 tsp dried oregano • 1/4 tsp sea salt (or to taste) • 1/8 tsp ground black pepper • 1 tbsp fresh parsley or basil, chopped (for garnish)	• **Calories:** 200 kcal • **Protein:** 3 g • **Carbohydrates:** 18 g • **Fats:** 14 g • **Fiber:** 6 g • **Cholesterol:** 0 mg • **Sodium:** 250 mg • **Potassium:** 500 mg

Equipment Needed
- Large skillet
- Wooden spoon
- Baking sheet (optional for toasting pine nuts)

Step-by-Step Instructions
Step 1: Prepare the Eggplant
1. Place the diced eggplant in a colander and sprinkle lightly with salt. Let sit for 10 minutes to draw out excess moisture and bitterness.
2. Rinse the eggplant under cool water and pat dry with a kitchen towel.

Step 2: Sauté the Vegetables
1. Heat 1 tbsp olive oil in a large skillet over medium heat.
2. Add the eggplant and sauté for 5–7 minutes, stirring occasionally, until lightly browned. Remove and set aside.
3. Add the remaining 1 tbsp olive oil to the skillet. Stir in the onion, celery, and garlic, and cook for 3–4 minutes until softened.

Step 3: Simmer the Caponata
1. Return the eggplant to the skillet and add the diced tomatoes, red wine vinegar, capers, oregano, sea salt, and black pepper.
2. Stir well and bring to a simmer. Reduce the heat to low, cover, and cook for 15 minutes, stirring occasionally, until the vegetables are tender and the flavors are well blended.

Step 4: Toast the Pine Nuts
1. While the caponata simmers, toast the pine nuts in a dry skillet over medium heat for 2–3 minutes or until golden and fragrant.

Step 5: Finish and Serve
1. Stir the toasted pine nuts into the caponata just before serving.
2. Garnish with fresh parsley or basil.

Serving Suggestions
- Serve warm or at room temperature as a side dish or appetizer.
- Pair with crusty whole-grain bread or pita for a delicious dip.
- Enjoy over quinoa or couscous for a hearty vegetarian meal.
- Use as a topping for grilled fish, chicken, or tofu.

4. Grilled Asparagus with Parmesan and Lemon Zest

Yield: 2 servings | **Preparation Time:** 10 minutes | **Cooking Time:** 8-10 minutes

Ingredients	Nutritional Information (Per Serving)
Base Ingredients • 1 bunch (about 1/2 lb) fresh asparagus, tough ends trimmed • 1 tbsp extra virgin olive oil • 1/4 tsp sea salt (or to taste) • 2 tbsp grated Parmesan cheese • 1 tsp fresh lemon zest • Optional: 1/4 tsp crushed red pepper flakes for a hint of spice	• **Calories:** 110 kcal • **Protein:** 4 g • **Carbohydrates:** 6 g • **Fats:** 8 g • **Cholesterol:** 5 mg • **Sodium:** 180 mg • **Potassium:** 200 mg

Equipment Needed
- Grill or grill pan
- Tongs or spatula
- Microplane or fine grater for zesting

Step-by-Step Instructions
Step 1: Prepare the Asparagus
1. Wash and trim the asparagus by snapping off the tough ends.
2. Pat dry with a kitchen towel.

Step 2: Season the Asparagus
1. toss the asparagus with olive oil, sea salt, and black pepper in a mixing bowl. Ensure each spear is evenly coated.

Step 3: Grill the Asparagus
1. Preheat a grill or grill pan over medium-high heat.
2. Arrange the asparagus spears in a single layer on the grill.
3. Grill for 4–5 minutes per side, turning occasionally with tongs, until tender and lightly charred.

Step 4: Add Parmesan and Lemon Zest
1. Transfer the grilled asparagus to a serving plate.
2. Sprinkle with grated Parmesan cheese and freshly grated lemon zest.
3. garnish with crushed red pepper flakes or fresh herbs if desired.

Serving Suggestions
- Serve alongside grilled fish, chicken, or steak for a complete Mediterranean meal.
- Pair with a quinoa or couscous salad for a light vegetarian dish.
- Add as a topping to pasta or whole-grain risotto for added texture and flavor.

This **Grilled Asparagus with Parmesan and Lemon Zest** recipe is a versatile side dish highlighting the Mediterranean Diet's emphasis on fresh, wholesome ingredients. It's a perfect balance of simplicity and sophistication, ideal for any meal. Enjoy!

5. Sautéed Green Beans with Garlic and Cherry Tomatoes

Yield: 2 servings | **Preparation Time:** 10 minutes | **Cooking Time:** 10 minutes

Ingredients	Nutritional Information (Per Serving)
Base Ingredients	• **Calories:** 100 kcal
• 1/2 lb (8 oz) fresh green beans, trimmed	• **Protein:** 2 g
• 1 cup cherry tomatoes, halved	• **Carbohydrates:** 8 g
• 2 garlic cloves, minced	• **Fats:** 7 g
• 1 tbsp extra virgin olive oil	• **Fiber:** 3 g
• 1/4 tsp sea salt (or to taste)	• **Cholesterol:** 0 mg
• 1/8 tsp ground black pepper	• **Sodium:** 150 mg
• 1/4 tsp crushed red pepper flakes (optional)	• **Potassium:** 250 mg
• 1 tsp fresh lemon juice (optional, for brightness)	

Equipment Needed
- Large skillet or sauté pan
- Wooden spoon or spatula

Step-by-Step Instructions
Step 1: Prepare the Green Beans
1. Wash the green beans and trim the ends.

Step 2: Blanch the Green Beans (Optional)
1. Bring a pot of salted water to a boil.
2. Add the green beans and blanch for 2 minutes.
3. Drain and immediately transfer to a bowl of ice water to stop cooking. Drain again.

Step 3: Sauté the Garlic
1. Heat the olive oil in a large skillet over medium heat.
2. Add the minced garlic and sauté for 30 seconds until fragrant, being careful not to let it burn.

Step 4: Cook the Green Beans and Tomatoes
1. Add the green beans to the skillet and sauté for 3–4 minutes, stirring occasionally.
2. Add the cherry tomatoes, sea salt, black pepper, and crushed red pepper flakes (if using).
3. cook for 3–4 minutes or until the tomatoes soften and the green beans are tender-crisp.

Step 5: Finish with Lemon Juice
1. Remove the skillet from the heat.
2. Drizzle with fresh lemon juice for added brightness (optional).

Serving Suggestions
- Serve alongside grilled chicken, fish, or lamb for a complete Mediterranean meal.
- Pair with quinoa, couscous, or whole-grain bread for a light vegetarian dish.
- Enjoy as a topping for pasta or rice bowls for added freshness and texture.

This **Sautéed Green Beans with Garlic and Cherry Tomatoes** is a simple yet flavorful dish that embodies the principles of the Mediterranean Diet. Fresh vegetables, heart-healthy olive oil, and aromatic garlic make it a standout addition to any table. Enjoy!

6. Stuffed Zucchini Boats with Couscous and Feta

Yield: 2 servings | **Preparation Time:** 15 minutes | **Chilling Time:** 25–30 minutes

Ingredients	Nutritional Information (Per Serving)
For the Zucchini Boats • 2 medium zucchini, halved lengthwise and seeds scooped out • 1 tbsp extra virgin olive oil • 1/4 tsp sea salt • 1/8 tsp ground black pepper **For the Couscous Filling** • 1/4 cup dry whole-grain couscous • 1/4 cup low-sodium vegetable broth or water • 1/4 cup diced cherry tomatoes • 1/4 cup canned chickpeas, rinsed and drained • 2 tbsp crumbled feta cheese • 1 tbsp chopped fresh parsley • 1 tbsp chopped fresh mint (optional) • 1 tsp fresh lemon juice • 1/4 tsp dried oregano • 1/4 tsp ground cumin • Pinch of red pepper flakes (optional)	• **Calories:** 220 kcal • **Protein:** 6 g • **Carbohydrates:** 20 g • **Fats:** 10 g • **Fiber:** 4 g • **Cholesterol:** 10 mg • **Sodium:** 200 mg • **Potassium:** 450 mg

Equipment Needed
- Baking dish
- Small saucepan
- Mixing bowl

Step-by-Step Instructions
Step 1: Prepare the Zucchini
1. Preheat the oven to 375°F (190°C).
2. Scoop out the seeds and some of the flesh from each zucchini half to create a hollow boat.
3. Brush the zucchini halves with olive oil and season with sea salt and black pepper.
4. Place them cut-side up in a baking dish.

Step 2: Cook the Couscous
1. bring the vegetable broth or water to a boil in a small saucepan.
2. Add the couscous, cover, and remove from heat. Let it sit for 5 minutes, then fluff it with a fork.

Step 3: Prepare the Filling
1. In a mixing bowl, combine the cooked couscous, diced tomatoes, chickpeas, feta cheese, parsley, mint (if using), lemon juice, oregano, cumin, and red pepper flakes (if using). Mix well.

Step 4: Stuff the Zucchini Boats
1. Spoon the couscous mixture evenly into the zucchini halves, pressing gently to pack the filling.

Step 5: Bake
1. Cover the baking dish with aluminum foil and bake for 20 minutes.
2. Remove the foil and bake for 5–10 minutes until the zucchini is tender and the filling is lightly browned.

Step 6: Serve

1. Garnish the stuffed zucchini boats with additional parsley or mint, if desired.

Serving Suggestions

- Serve alongside a crisp green salad with a lemon-olive oil vinaigrette.
- Pair with grilled chicken or fish for a hearty meal.
- Enjoy as a standalone vegetarian dish with a dollop of Greek yogurt.

---

7. Baked Sweet Potatoes with a Herb Yogurt Sauce

Yield: 2 servings | **Preparation Time:** 10 minutes | **Cooking Time:** 40–45 minutes

Ingredients	Nutritional Information (Per Serving)
For the Baked Sweet Potatoes • 2 medium sweet potatoes (about 6 oz each), scrubbed and patted dry • 1 tbsp extra virgin olive oil • 1/4 tsp sea salt • 1/8 tsp ground black pepper **For the Herb Yogurt Sauce** • 1/2 cup plain Greek yogurt • 1 tbsp fresh parsley, chopped • 1 tbsp fresh dill, chopped • 1 tsp fresh lemon juice • 1/2 tsp lemon zest • 1 small garlic clove, minced • 1/8 tsp sea salt (or to taste) • 1/8 tsp ground black pepper	• **Calories:** 220 kcal • **Protein:** 6 g • **Carbohydrates:** 33 g • **Fats:** 7 g • **Fiber:** 5 g • **Cholesterol:** 5 mg • **Sodium:** 200 mg • **Potassium:** 450 mg

Equipment Needed
- Baking sheet
- Mixing bowl
- Fork or potato masher

Step-by-Step Instructions

Step 1: Prepare the Sweet Potatoes
1. Preheat the oven to 400°F (200°C).
2. Pierce each sweet potato a few times with a fork to allow steam to escape during baking.
3. Rub the sweet potatoes with olive oil and season with sea salt and black pepper.

Step 2: Bake the Sweet Potatoes
1. Place the sweet potatoes on a baking sheet lined with parchment paper or foil.
2. Bake for 40–45 minutes or until the sweet potatoes are tender when pierced with a fork.

Step 3: Make the Herb Yogurt Sauce
1. In a mixing bowl, combine Greek yogurt, parsley, dill, lemon juice, lemon zest, garlic, sea salt, and black pepper.
2. Mix well until smooth and creamy. Adjust seasoning to taste.

Step 4: Assemble the Dish
1. Once the sweet potatoes are baked, slice them open lengthwise to create a pocket.
2. Fluff the interior slightly with a fork and spoon the herb yogurt sauce generously over the top.

Step 5: Garnish and Serve
1. Garnish with additional chopped herbs or a sprinkle of smoked paprika, if desired.

Serving Suggestions
- Pair with a side of sautéed spinach or a fresh green salad for a light meal.
- Serve alongside grilled chicken or fish for a more substantial Mediterranean-inspired dinner.
- Enjoy as a satisfying vegetarian main or a flavorful side dish.

This **Baked Sweet Potatoes with a Herb Yogurt Sauce** recipe is a wholesome and versatile dish that highlights the simplicity and richness of the Mediterranean Diet. Its sweet, tangy, and savory flavors make it a perfect choice for any occasion. Enjoy!

1. Creamy Tomato Basil Soup with Olive Oil Drizzle

Yield: 2 servings | **Preparation Time:** 10 minutes | **Cooking Time:** 30 minutes

Ingredients	Nutritional Information (Per Serving)
For the Soup <ul><li>4 large ripe tomatoes (about 1 lb), chopped</li><li>1 small onion, finely chopped</li><li>2 garlic cloves, minced</li><li>1 tbsp extra virgin olive oil</li><li>1/2 cup low-sodium vegetable broth</li><li>1/4 cup unsweetened almond milk (or any milk of choice)</li><li>2 tbsp tomato paste</li><li>1/2 tsp dried oregano</li><li>1/4 tsp crushed red pepper flakes (optional, for spice)</li><li>1/4 cup fresh basil leaves, chopped (plus more for garnish)</li></ul> **For the Olive Oil Drizzle** <ul><li>1 tbsp extra virgin olive oil</li><li>1/4 tsp smoked paprika or crushed red pepper flakes (optional, for garnish)</li></ul>	<ul><li>**Calories:** 150 kcal</li><li>**Protein:** 3 g</li><li>**Carbohydrates:** 12 g</li><li>**Fats:** 10 g</li><li>**Fiber:** 3 g</li><li>**Cholesterol:** 0 mg</li><li>**Sodium:** 180 mg</li><li>**Potassium:** 400 mg</li></ul>

Equipment Needed
- Large pot or saucepan
- Immersion blender or regular blender
- Ladle

Step-by-Step Instructions
Step 1: Sauté the Aromatics
1. Heat the olive oil in a large pot over medium heat.
2. Add the onion and sauté for 3–4 minutes until softened.
3. Stir in the garlic and cook for 1 minute until fragrant.

Step 2: Simmer the Soup
1. Add the chopped tomatoes, vegetable broth, tomato paste, oregano, sea salt, black pepper, and crushed red pepper flakes (if using).
2. Stir well and bring to a simmer.
3. Reduce the heat to low and cover the pot. Simmer for 20 minutes, stirring occasionally.

Step 3: Blend and Add Creaminess
1. Remove the pot from heat and let it cool slightly.
2. Blend the soup until smooth using an immersion blender. Alternatively, transfer it to a regular blender and blend in batches, then return it to the pot.
3. Stir in the almond milk and chopped basil. Heat gently for 2–3 minutes, but do not let it boil.

Step 4: Prepare the Olive Oil Drizzle
1. In a small bowl, mix the olive oil with smoked paprika or crushed red pepper flakes (if desired).

Step 5: Serve
1. Ladle the soup into bowls and drizzle with the prepared olive oil.
2. Garnish with additional fresh basil leaves.

Serving Suggestions
- Pair with a slice of crusty whole-grain bread or whole-grain croutons.
- Serve alongside a simple green salad with a lemon-olive oil vinaigrette.
- Enjoy as a starter or light meal with grilled vegetables or a small portion of roasted chicken.

This **Creamy Tomato Basil Soup with Olive Oil Drizzle** is a perfect example of Mediterranean cuisine's focus on fresh, wholesome ingredients and heart-healthy fats. It's a nourishing and delicious option for any occasion. Enjoy!

2. Lentil and Spinach Soup with Lemon

Yield: 2 servings | **Preparation Time:** 10 minutes | **Cooking Time:** 30 minutes

Ingredients	Nutritional Information (Per Serving)
For the Soup • 1/2 cup dry green or brown lentils, rinsed and drained • 1 tbsp extra virgin olive oil • 1 small onion, finely chopped • 1 small carrot, peeled and diced • 1 celery stalk, diced • 2 garlic cloves, minced • 3 cups low-sodium vegetable broth • 1/2 tsp ground cumin • 1/4 tsp ground turmeric • 1/4 tsp sea salt (or to taste) • 1/8 tsp ground black pepper • 2 cups fresh spinach, roughly chopped • 1 tbsp fresh lemon juice (or to taste) • Lemon wedges (for garnish) **Optional Customizations** • Add 1/4 tsp red pepper flakes for a touch of spice. • Include 1/4 cup diced tomatoes for extra flavor. • Substitute spinach with kale or Swiss chard.	• **Calories:** 210 kcal • **Protein:** 12 g • **Carbohydrates:** 28 g • **Fats:** 5 g • **Fiber:** 8 g • **Cholesterol:** 0 mg • **Sodium:** 200 mg • **Potassium:** 400 mg

Equipment Needed

• Medium pot
• Wooden spoon

- Ladle

Step-by-Step Instructions
Step 1: Sauté the Aromatics
1. Heat the olive oil in a medium pot over medium heat.
2. Add the onion, carrot, and celery. Sauté for 4–5 minutes until softened.
3. Stir in the garlic and cook for 1 minute until fragrant.

Step 2: Cook the Lentils
1. Add the lentils, vegetable broth, cumin, turmeric, sea salt, and black pepper to the pot. Stir to combine.
2. Bring the mixture to a boil, then reduce the heat to low and cover. Simmer for 20–25 minutes or until the lentils are tender.

Step 3: Add the Spinach
1. Stir in the chopped spinach and let it wilt for 2–3 minutes.
2. Add the lemon juice and adjust the seasoning with additional salt and pepper, if needed.

Step 4: Serve
1. Ladle the soup into bowls and garnish with lemon wedges for squeezing.

Serving Suggestions
- Serve with a slice of crusty whole-grain bread or pita for dipping.
- Pair with a simple green salad with olive oil and balsamic dressing.
- Enjoy as a light meal or a hearty starter for a Mediterranean-inspired dinner.

This **Lentil and Spinach Soup with Lemon** highlights the health benefits of lentils, fresh greens, and vibrant Mediterranean flavors. It's a wholesome, nutrient-packed dish that's perfect for any occasion. Enjoy!

3. Chickpea and Vegetable Minestrone

Yield: 2 servings | **Preparation Time:** 15 minutes | **Cooking Time:** 30 minutes

Ingredients	Nutritional Information (Per Serving)
For the Soup - 1 tbsp extra virgin olive oil - 1 small onion, diced - 1 small carrot, peeled and diced - 1 celery stalk, diced - 1 garlic clove, minced - 1 small zucchini, diced - 1 cup canned diced tomatoes (no salt added) - 2 cups low-sodium vegetable broth - 1/2 cup cooked chickpeas (or canned, rinsed and drained) - 1/2 cup small pasta (like ditalini or elbow macaroni) - 1/2 tsp dried oregano - 1/2 tsp dried basil - 1/4 tsp sea salt (or to taste) - 1/8 tsp ground black pepper - 1/4 cup fresh spinach or kale, chopped (optional)	- **Calories:** 280 kcal - **Protein:** 8 g - **Carbohydrates:** 38 g - **Fats:** 7 g - **Fiber:** 8 g - **Cholesterol:** 0 mg - **Sodium:** 220 mg - **Potassium:** 450 mg

Equipment Needed
- Large pot or Dutch oven
- Wooden spoon
- Ladle

Step-by-Step Instructions

Step 1: Sauté the Aromatics
1. Heat olive oil in a large pot over medium heat.
2. Add the onion, carrot, celery, and sauté for 4–5 minutes until softened.
3. Stir in the garlic and cook for 1 minute until fragrant.

Step 2: Add the Vegetables and Broth
1. Add the zucchini, diced tomatoes, and vegetable broth to the pot.
2. Stir in the oregano, basil, sea salt, and black pepper.
3. Bring to a boil, reduce the heat to low, and simmer for 10 minutes.

Step 3: Add the Chickpeas and Pasta
1. Stir in the chickpeas and pasta.
2. Simmer for 10–12 minutes or until the pasta is cooked and tender.
3. If using spinach or kale, stir it in during the last 2 minutes of cooking.

Step 4: Adjust Seasoning
1. Taste and adjust the seasoning with additional salt and pepper, if needed.

Step 5: Serve
1. Ladle the minestrone into bowls and drizzle with extra virgin olive oil for added richness.
2. Garnish with fresh herbs or grated Parmesan cheese, if desired.

Serving Suggestions

- Serve with crusty whole-grain bread for dipping.
- Pair with a side of roasted vegetables or a fresh salad.
- Enjoy as a main course or as a starter to a Mediterranean-inspired meal.

This **Chickpea and Vegetable Minestrone** showcases the Mediterranean Diet's emphasis on fresh vegetables, legumes, and wholesome flavors. It's a comforting and versatile dish perfect for any occasion. Enjoy!

4. Roasted Red Pepper and Tomato Soup

Yield: 2 servings | **Preparation Time:** 15 minutes | **Cooking Time:** 30 minutes

Ingredients	Nutritional Information (Per Serving)
Base Ingredients • 2 large red bell peppers, halved and seeds removed • 4 large ripe tomatoes, halved • 1 small onion, chopped • 2 garlic cloves, peeled • 1 tbsp extra virgin olive oil • 2 cups low-sodium vegetable broth • 1/4 tsp smoked paprika • 1/2 tsp dried oregano • 1/4 tsp sea salt (or to taste) • 1/8 tsp ground black pepper • 1 tbsp fresh basil, chopped (plus more for garnish) • 1 tsp balsamic vinegar (optional, for extra depth)	• **Calories:** 150 kcal • **Protein:** 4 g • **Carbohydrates:** 20 g • **Fats:** 6 g • **Fiber:** 5 g • **Cholesterol:** 0 mg • **Sodium:** 180 mg • **Potassium:** 500 mg

Equipment Needed

- Baking sheet

107

- Large pot
- Immersion blender or regular blender

Step-by-Step Instructions
Step 1: Roast the Vegetables
1. Preheat the oven to 400°F (200°C).
2. Place the red bell peppers, tomatoes (cut side up), onion, and garlic on a baking sheet.
3. Drizzle with olive oil and sprinkle with smoked paprika, oregano, sea salt, and black pepper.
4. Roast in the oven for 20–25 minutes or until the peppers are slightly charred and the tomatoes are softened.

Step 2: Blend the Vegetables
1. Remove the roasted vegetables from the oven and let them cool slightly.
2. Transfer the roasted vegetables to a blender or use an immersion blender in a pot. Add the vegetable broth and blend until smooth.

Step 3: Simmer the Soup
1. Place the blended mixture into a large pot over medium heat.
2. Stir in the balsamic vinegar (if using) and fresh basil. Simmer for 5–10 minutes to let the flavors meld.

Step 4: Adjust Seasoning
1. Taste and adjust the seasoning with additional salt, pepper, or smoked paprika, if needed.

Step 5: Serve
1. Ladle the soup into bowls and drizzle with extra virgin olive oil.
2. Garnish with fresh basil leaves or a sprinkle of red pepper flakes for added flavor.

Serving Suggestions
- Serve with a side of crusty whole-grain bread for dipping.
- Pair with a fresh Mediterranean salad or grilled vegetables for a complete meal.
- Enjoy as a starter to a Mediterranean-inspired dinner.

This **Roasted Red Pepper and Tomato Soup** combines the bold flavors of roasted vegetables with Mediterranean herbs and spices. It's a healthy and delicious choice for any occasion. Enjoy!

5. Seafood Chowder with Mediterranean Spices

Yield: 2 servings | **Preparation Time:** 15 minutes | **Cooking Time:** 30 minutes

Ingredients	Nutritional Information (Per Serving)
Base Ingredients • 1 tbsp extra virgin olive oil • 1 small onion, finely chopped • 1 small carrot, diced • 1 celery stalk, diced • 2 garlic cloves, minced • 1/2 tsp smoked paprika • 1/2 tsp dried thyme • 1/2 tsp dried oregano • 1/4 tsp crushed red pepper flakes (optional, for heat) • 2 cups low-sodium fish or vegetable broth • 1/2 cup unsweetened almond milk (or low-fat milk) • 1 small potato, peeled and diced • 1/2 cup canned diced tomatoes (no salt added) • 1/4 lb white fish fillet (such as cod or haddock), cut into 1-inch pieces • 1/4 lb peeled and deveined shrimp • 1 tbsp fresh parsley, chopped (plus more for garnish) • 1/2 tsp sea salt (or to taste) • 1/8 tsp ground black pepper	• **Calories:** 230 kcal • **Protein:** 24 g • **Carbohydrates:** 15 g • **Fats:** 8 g • **Fiber:** 3 g • **Cholesterol:** 110 mg • **Sodium:** 300 mg • **Potassium:** 550 mg

Equipment Needed
- Large pot or Dutch oven
- Wooden spoon
- Ladle

Step-by-Step Instructions

Step 1: Sauté the Vegetables
1. Heat olive oil in a large pot over medium heat.
2. Add the onion, carrot, celery, and sauté for 4–5 minutes until softened.
3. Stir in the garlic, smoked paprika, thyme, oregano, and crushed red pepper flakes (if using). Cook for 1 minute until fragrant.

Step 2: Simmer the Broth
1. Add the diced potatoes, tomatoes, and fish or vegetable broth to the pot.
2. Bring to a boil, then reduce the heat to low. Cover and simmer for 15 minutes or until the potatoes are tender.

Step 3: Add the Seafood
1. Stir in the white fish and shrimp.
2. Simmer gently for 5–7 minutes until the fish is opaque and flakes easily with a fork, and the shrimp are pink and cooked through.

Step 4: Add the Creamy Element
1. Stir in the almond milk and heat gently for 2–3 minutes. Do not boil.
2. Season with sea salt and black pepper to taste.

Step 5: Serve
1. Ladle the chowder into bowls and garnish with fresh parsley.

Serving Suggestions
- Serve with a side of crusty whole-grain bread for dipping.
- Pair with a simple green salad or roasted vegetables.
- Enjoy as a light meal or starter for a Mediterranean-inspired feast.

This **Seafood Chowder with Mediterranean Spices** perfectly blends hearty ingredients and light, fresh flavors. It's a delicious way to enjoy the health benefits of seafood and Mediterranean cuisine. Enjoy!

6. Saffron and Leek Soup with Barley

Yield: 2 servings | Preparation Time: 10 minutes | Chilling Time: 35–40 minutes

Ingredients	Nutritional Information (Per Serving)
Base Ingredients • 1 tbsp extra virgin olive oil • 1 medium leek, white and light green parts only, sliced into thin rounds • 1 small carrot, peeled and diced • 1 small celery stalk, diced • 1 garlic clove, minced • 1/4 cup pearled barley, rinsed • 1/8 tsp saffron threads, dissolved in 2 tbsp warm water • 3 cups low-sodium vegetable broth • 1/4 tsp dried thyme • 1/4 tsp ground turmeric (optional, for color and flavor) • 1/4 tsp sea salt (or to taste) • 1/8 tsp ground black pepper • 1 tbsp fresh parsley, chopped (plus more for garnish) • Lemon wedges for serving	• **Calories:** 180 kcal • **Protein:** 4 g • **Carbohydrates:** 25 g • **Fats:** 6 g • **Fiber:** 5 g • **Cholesterol:** 0 mg • **Sodium:** 180 mg • **Potassium:** 450 mg

Equipment Needed
- Medium pot
- Wooden spoon
- Ladle

111

Step-by-Step Instructions
Step 1: Prepare the Saffron
1.   Dissolve the saffron threads in 2 tablespoons of warm water and set aside.

Step 2: Sauté the Vegetables
1.   Heat olive oil in a medium pot over medium heat.
2.   Add the sliced leeks, carrots, and celery. Sauté for 5–6 minutes until softened.
3.   Stir in the garlic and cook for 1 minute until fragrant.

Step 3: Add the Barley and Broth
1.   Add the rinsed barley to the pot, stirring to combine with the vegetables.
2.   Pour in the vegetable broth and bring to a gentle boil.
3.   Reduce the heat to low, cover, and simmer for 20 minutes, stirring occasionally.

Step 4: Add the Saffron and Seasonings
1.   Stir in the saffron water, thyme, turmeric (if using), sea salt, and black pepper.
2.   Continue simmering for 10–15 minutes or until the barley is tender.

Step 5: Finish the Soup
1.   Stir in the chopped parsley and adjust the seasoning to taste.

Step 6: Serve
1.   Ladle the soup into bowls and garnish with additional parsley.
2.   Serve with a wedge of lemon on the side for a fresh citrus burst.

Serving Suggestions
- Pair with a slice of crusty whole-grain bread or pita for dipping.
- Serve as a light main course or alongside a fresh Mediterranean salad.
- Top with olive oil or a sprinkle of Parmesan for extra richness.

This **Saffron and Leek Soup with Barley** is a perfect example of Mediterranean cuisine's focus on wholesome ingredients, delicate flavors, and vibrant spices. It's a comforting and healthful dish to enjoy any time of the year. Enjoy!

7. Traditional Greek Avgolemono Soup

Yield: 2 servings | **Preparation Time:** 10 minutes | **Cooking Time:** 25 minutes

Ingredients	Nutritional Information (Per Serving)
For the Soup • 3 cups low-sodium chicken broth or vegetable broth • 1/4 cup uncooked white rice or orzo pasta • 1 egg • 2 tbsp fresh lemon juice (about 1 medium lemon) • 1 small carrot, peeled and diced (optional) • 1 celery stalk, diced (optional) • 1/4 tsp sea salt (or to taste) • 1/8 tsp ground black pepper • 1 tbsp fresh parsley, chopped (for garnish)	• **Calories:** 150 kcal • **Protein:** 6 g • **Carbohydrates:** 20 g • **Fats:** 5 g • **Fiber:** 1 g • **Cholesterol:** 70 mg • **Sodium:** 250 mg • **Potassium:** 300 mg

Equipment Needed
- Medium pot
- Whisk
- Ladle

Step-by-Step Instructions

Step 1: Cook the Base Soup
1. bring the chicken or vegetable broth to a boil in a medium pot.
2. Add the rice (or orzo) and reduce the heat to low. Simmer for 15 minutes or until the rice is tender.
3. Add diced carrot and celery to the pot at this stage and cook until softened.

Step 2: Prepare the Avgolemono Mixture
1. In a medium bowl, whisk the egg until frothy.
2. Gradually whisk in the lemon juice.

Step 3: Temper the Egg Mixture
1. Remove the pot from heat.
2. Slowly ladle about 1/2 cup of the hot broth into the egg-lemon mixture while whisking constantly. This prevents the eggs from curdling.
3. Gradually pour the tempered egg mixture back into the pot, whisking as you pour.

Step 4: Finish the Soup
1. Return the pot to low heat and warm the soup gently, stirring occasionally, for 2–3 minutes. Do not let the soup boil, as this may curdle the egg.
2. Season with sea salt and black pepper to taste.

Step 5: Serve
1. Ladle the soup into bowls and garnish with fresh parsley.

2. Serve with a wedge of lemon on the side for extra brightness.

Serving Suggestions
- Pair with crusty whole-grain bread or a Greek salad for a complete meal.
- Serve as a light starter for a Mediterranean-inspired dinner.
- Enjoy with a drizzle of olive oil or a sprinkle of Parmesan for added richness.

This **Traditional Greek Avgolemono Soup** is a perfect blend of creamy, tangy, and hearty flavors that highlights the simplicity and richness of Mediterranean cuisine. It's a nutritious and satisfying dish perfect for any season. Enjoy!

1. Greek Baklava with Honey and Walnuts

Yield: 2 servings (about 4 small pieces) | **Preparation Time:** 20 minutes | **Cooking Time:** 30 minutes

Ingredients	Nutritional Information (Per Serving)
For the Baklava • 6 sheets phyllo dough (thawed according to package instructions) • 1/4 cup walnuts, finely chopped • 1/4 tsp ground cinnamon • 1/8 tsp ground cloves (optional) • 2 tbsp extra virgin olive oil or melted unsalted butter **For the Honey Syrup** • 2 tbsp honey • 2 tbsp water • 1 tsp fresh lemon juice • 1 small cinnamon stick (optional)	• **Calories:** 180 kcal • **Protein:** 3 g • **Carbohydrates:** 20 g • **Fats:** 10 g • **Fiber:** 2 g • **Cholesterol:** 0 mg • **Sodium:** 20 mg • **Potassium:** 60 mg

Equipment Needed
- Small baking dish (approximately 6x6 inches)
- Pastry brush
- Small saucepan

Step-by-Step Instructions
Step 1: Prepare the Filling
1. Mix the chopped walnuts, ground cinnamon, and ground cloves (if using) in a small bowl.

Step 2: Assemble the Baklava
1. Preheat the oven to 350°F (175°C).
2. Brush a small baking dish with olive oil or melted butter.
3. Place one sheet of phyllo dough in the dish, letting the edges hang over. Brush the top with olive oil or butter. Repeat with two more sheets, brushing each layer.
4. Spread half of the walnut mixture evenly over the phyllo.
5. Add three layers of phyllo, brushing each with olive oil or butter.
6. Spread the remaining walnut mixture on top.
7. Finish with the remaining phyllo sheets, brushing each with olive oil or butter.
8. Tuck the edges of the phyllo neatly into the pan. Cut the baklava into small diamond or square shapes using a sharp knife.

Step 3: Bake the Baklava
1. Place the dish in the oven and bake for 25–30 minutes or until the phyllo is golden and crisp.

Step 4: Make the Honey Syrup
1. While the baklava bakes, combine honey, water, lemon juice, and the cinnamon stick (if using) in a small saucepan.
2. Heat over low-medium heat, stirring occasionally, until the syrup thickens slightly (about 5 minutes). Remove from heat and set aside.

Step 5: Add the Syrup
1. Once the baklava is baked, remove it from the oven and drizzle the warm syrup evenly over the top.
2. Let the baklava rest for at least 15 minutes to allow the syrup to soak in.

Step 6: Serve
1. Carefully remove the baklava pieces from the pan using a spatula.
2. Garnish with a drizzle of honey or a sprinkle of chopped nuts, if desired.

Serving Suggestions
*   Enjoy Greek coffee or mint tea as a dessert or a special treat.
*   Serve with a dollop of plain Greek yogurt for a creamy complement.
*   Store leftovers in an airtight container at room temperature for 3 days.

This **Greek Baklava with Honey and Walnuts** is a healthier take on the traditional dessert. It uses heart-healthy olive oil and a touch of natural sweetness from honey. It's a delightful way to indulge in Mediterranean flavors! Enjoy!

2. Lemon Olive Oil Cake with Fresh Berries

Yield: 2 servings | **Preparation Time:** 10 minutes | **Cooking Time:** 25–30 minutes

Ingredients	Nutritional Information (Per Serving)
For the Cake • 1/3 cup all-purpose flour • 1/4 tsp baking powder • 1/8 tsp baking soda • Pinch of sea salt • 1 large egg • 2 tbsp extra virgin olive oil • 2 tbsp honey (or maple syrup) • 1 tbsp fresh lemon juice • 1/2 tsp lemon zest • 2 tbsp unsweetened almond milk (or any milk of choice) **For the Berry Topping** • 1/2 cup mixed fresh berries (e.g., blueberries, raspberries, or sliced strawberries) • 1 tsp honey (optional, for sweetness) • 1/2 tsp fresh lemon juice **Optional Customizations** • Add 1/4 tsp vanilla extract to the cake batter for a richer flavor. • Substitute almond flour for a gluten-free option. • Sprinkle with a pinch of powdered sugar or drizzle with a little honey before serving.	• **Calories:** 210 kcal • **Protein:** 4 g • **Carbohydrates:** 24 g • **Fats:** 10 g • **Fiber:** 2 g • **Cholesterol:** 60 mg • **Sodium:** 90 mg • **Potassium:** 150 mg

Equipment Needed
- Small mixing bowls
- Whisk
- 4-inch round or square baking dish (or ramekins)
- Oven

Step-by-Step Instructions
Step 1: Preheat the Oven
1. Preheat your oven to 350°F (175°C).
2. Lightly grease a small baking dish or ramekins with olive oil.

Step 2: Mix the Dry Ingredients
1. Whisk together the flour, baking powder, baking soda, and sea salt in a small bowl.

Step 3: Mix the Wet Ingredients
1. In another bowl, whisk the egg, olive oil, honey, lemon juice, lemon zest, and almond milk until smooth.

Step 4: Combine the Batter
1. Gradually fold the dry ingredients into the wet ingredients, stirring gently until combined. Do not overmix.

Step 5: Bake the Cake
1. Pour the batter into the prepared baking dish or ramekins.
2. Bake for 25–30 minutes or until a toothpick inserted into the center comes clean.
3. Remove from the oven and let cool slightly.

Step 6: Prepare the Berry Topping
1. toss the fresh berries with honey and lemon juice in a small bowl. Set aside for a few minutes to allow the flavors to meld.

Step 7: Serve
1. Carefully remove the cake from the dish or ramekins and place it on a serving plate.
2. Top with the fresh berry mixture.
3. Garnish with a sprinkle of powdered sugar or a drizzle of honey, if desired.

Serving Suggestions
- Enjoy as a light dessert or a sweet treat with tea or coffee.
- Pair with a dollop of Greek yogurt for added creaminess.
- Serve with a drizzle of balsamic glaze for a unique flavor twist.

This **Lemon Olive Oil Cake with Fresh Berries** is a delightful dessert that showcases the vibrant flavors of the Mediterranean. Its light texture and bright citrus notes make it a perfect way to indulge while staying true to a healthy lifestyle. Enjoy!

3. Pistachio and Cardamom Biscotti

Yield: 2 servings (4–6 biscotti) | **Preparation Time:** 15 minutes | **Cooking Time:** 25-30 minutes

Ingredients	Nutritional Information (Per Serving)
For the Biscotti • 1/2 cup all-purpose flour (or whole-wheat flour for added fiber) • 1/4 tsp baking powder • 1/8 tsp ground cardamom • Pinch of sea salt • 1 tbsp honey (or maple syrup) • 1 small egg, lightly beaten • 1 tbsp extra virgin olive oil • 1/4 cup shelled unsalted pistachios, chopped • 1/4 tsp vanilla extract (optional)	• **Calories:** 180 kcal • **Protein:** 5 g • **Carbohydrates:** 20 g • **Fats:** 8 g • **Fiber:** 2 g • **Cholesterol:** 30 mg • **Sodium:** 60 mg • **Potassium:** 100 mg

Equipment Needed
- Mixing bowls
- Whisk
- Baking sheet
- Parchment paper
- Sharp knife

Step-by-Step Instructions
Step 1: Preheat the Oven
1. Preheat your oven to 350°F (175°C).
2. Line a baking sheet with parchment paper.

Step 2: Mix the Dry Ingredients

1. Mix the flour, baking powder, cardamom, and sea salt in a medium bowl.

Step 3: Mix the Wet Ingredients

1. In a separate bowl, combine the honey, egg, olive oil, and vanilla extract (if using). Whisk until smooth.

Step 4: Combine the Dough

1. Gradually add the dry ingredients to the wet ingredients, stirring until a sticky dough forms.
2. Fold in the chopped pistachios.

Step 5: Shape the Biscotti

1. On the prepared baking sheet, shape the dough into a flat log about 1 inch high and 4 inches long.
2. Smooth the edges with damp hands to ensure even baking.

Step 6: First Bake

1. Bake the log in the preheated oven for 15–18 minutes or until it is firm to the touch and lightly golden.
2. Remove from the oven and let it cool for 5 minutes.

Step 7: Slice and Second Bake

1. Using a sharp knife, slice the log into 1/2-inch-thick pieces on a slight diagonal.
2. Arrange the slices cut-side down on the baking sheet.
3. Bake for an additional 8–10 minutes, flipping halfway through, until the biscotti are crisp and golden.

Step 8: Cool and Serve

1. Transfer the biscotti to a wire rack to cool completely.

Serving Suggestions

- Enjoy as a snack or dessert with coffee, tea, or a glass of almond milk.
- Serve alongside a bowl of Greek yogurt with honey for a Mediterranean-inspired breakfast.
- Drizzle with a bit of melted dark chocolate for an indulgent treat.

4. Yogurt Parfaits with Pomegranate and Granola

Yield: 2 servings | **Preparation Time:** 10 minutes | **Cooking Time:** None

Ingredients	Nutritional Information (Per Serving)
Base Ingredients - 1 cup plain Greek yogurt (2% fat or your preference) - 1/4 cup pomegranate seeds - 1/4 cup granola (choose a whole-grain, low-sugar variety) - 1 tbsp honey or maple syrup (optional, for sweetness) **Optional Customizations** - Add 1 tbsp chopped nuts (e.g., almonds, walnuts, or pistachios) for crunch. - Layer in 1/4 cup fresh berries (e.g., blueberries or raspberries) for extra flavor. - Sprinkle with a pinch of ground cinnamon or nutmeg for a warm, aromatic twist.	- **Calories:** 200 kcal - **Protein:** 8 g - **Carbohydrates:** 28 g - **Fats:** 5 g - **Fiber:** 3 g - **Cholesterol:** 5 mg - **Sodium:** 60 mg - **Potassium:** 200 mg

Equipment Needed
- Two glasses, jars, or bowls for serving
- Spoon for layering

Step-by-Step Instructions
Step 1: Prepare the Ingredients
1. Gather and measure all the ingredients.
2. Using fresh pomegranate, remove the seeds by cutting the fruit in half and tapping the back with a spoon over a bowl.

Step 2: Sweeten the Yogurt (Optional)
1. If you prefer sweeter yogurt, mix the Greek yogurt with honey or maple syrup in a small bowl.

Step 3: Layer the Parfait
1. Add 2 tbsp of Greek yogurt as the base layer in the serving glass or bowl.
2. Add 1 tbsp of granola as the second layer.
3. Sprinkle 1 tbsp of pomegranate seeds on top of the granola.
4. Repeat the layers until the glass is full, ending with a topping of pomegranate seeds and a sprinkle of granola.

Step 4: Garnish and Serve
1. Garnish the top with a drizzle of honey, a sprinkle of cinnamon, or a few chopped nuts (optional).
2. Serve immediately with a spoon.

Serving Suggestions
- Pair with a cup of mint or green tea for a light Mediterranean-inspired breakfast.
- Enjoy as a refreshing snack on a warm day.
- Serve in small portions as a healthy dessert option after dinner.

This **Yogurt Parfaits with Pomegranate and Granola** recipe is a delicious and nutritious way to enjoy the flavors of the Mediterranean Diet. Its balance of protein, healthy fats, and antioxidants makes it perfect for a wide range of dietary preferences. Enjoy!

5. Orange and Almond Flourless Cake

Yield: 2 servings **|** **Preparation Time:** 15 minutes **|** **Cooking Time:** 40–45 minutes

Ingredients	Nutritional Information (Per Serving)
For the Cake • 1 medium orange (about 6 oz) • 1 large egg • 1/4 cup almond flour • 2 tbsp honey or maple syrup • 1/4 tsp baking powder • 1/8 tsp ground cinnamon (optional) • Pinch of sea salt **Optional Customizations** • Add 1/4 tsp vanilla extract for extra flavor. • Sprinkle with slivered almonds on top before baking for added texture. • Dust with powdered sugar or drizzle with honey for a finishing touch.	• **Calories:** 220 kcal • **Protein:** 6 g • **Carbohydrates:** 20 g • **Fats:** 12 g • **Fiber:** 4 g • **Cholesterol:** 70 mg • **Sodium:** 50 mg • **Potassium:** 200 mg

Equipment Needed
- Small saucepan
- Blender or food processor
- Small mixing bowl

- 4-inch round baking dish or ramekin
- Oven

Step-by-Step Instructions

Step 1: Prepare the Orange
1. Place the orange in a small saucepan and cover it with water.
2. Bring to a boil, then reduce the heat and simmer for 20 minutes or until the orange is soft.
3. Remove the orange from the water and let it cool.

Step 2: Preheat the Oven
1. Preheat your oven to 350°F (175°C).
2. Grease a small baking dish or ramekin with olive oil or line it with parchment paper.

Step 3: Blend the Wet Ingredients
1. Cut the cooled orange into quarters, removing any seeds but keeping the peel.
2. Add the orange quarters to a blender or food processor.
3. Blend with the egg and honey until smooth.

Step 4: Combine the Dry Ingredients
1. In a small bowl, mix the almond flour, baking powder, cinnamon (if using), and a pinch of salt.

Step 5: Make the Batter
1. Pour the orange mixture into the dry ingredients and stir until combined.
2. Transfer the batter to the prepared baking dish.

Step 6: Bake the Cake
1. Bake for 40–45 minutes or until a toothpick inserted into the center comes clean.
2. Remove from the oven and let cool in the dish for 10 minutes before transferring to a plate.

Step 7: Serve
1. Serve slices of the cake warm or at room temperature.
2. Garnish with a drizzle of honey, a sprinkle of slivered almonds, or a dollop of Greek yogurt.

Serving Suggestions
- Pair with a cup of chamomile tea or espresso for a Mediterranean-style treat.
- Serve with fresh fruit, such as berries or orange slices, for added brightness.
- Enjoy as a light dessert or a midday snack.

This **Orange and Almond Flourless Cake** highlights the Mediterranean Diet's use of simple, wholesome ingredients. It's a fragrant and satisfying dessert that's both gluten-free and naturally sweetened. Enjoy!

6. Honey-Soaked Semolina Cake with Pistachios

Yield: 2 servings | **Preparation Time:** 15 minutes | **Chilling Time:** 30–35 minutes

Ingredients	Nutritional Information (Per Serving)
For the Cake • 1/4 cup fine semolina • 2 tbsp all-purpose flour (or almond flour for a gluten-free option) • 1/8 tsp baking powder • Pinch of sea salt • 1 tbsp plain Greek yogurt • 1 tbsp extra virgin olive oil • 1 tbsp honey • 1/8 tsp ground cardamom (optional, for a warm flavor) • 2 tbsp milk (dairy or plant-based) **For the Honey Syrup** • 2 tbsp honey • 2 tbsp water • 1/2 tsp fresh lemon juice • 1/8 tsp orange blossom water or rose water (optional, for fragrance) **For the Garnish** • 1 tbsp chopped unsalted pistachios • 1/8 tsp ground cinnamon (optional)	• **Calories:** 210 kcal • **Protein:** 4 g • **Carbohydrates:** 28 g • **Fats:** 8 g • **Fiber:** 1 g • **Cholesterol:** 5 mg • **Sodium:** 50 mg • **Potassium:** 120 mg

Equipment Needed

• Small mixing bowl

- Whisk or spoon
- Small baking dish or ramekins
- Saucepan

Step-by-Step Instructions
Step 1: Preheat the Oven
1. Preheat your oven to 350°F (175°C).
2. Grease a small baking dish or ramekins with olive oil.

Step 2: Mix the Dry Ingredients
1. In a small bowl, combine the semolina, flour, baking powder, sea salt, and ground cardamom (if using).

Step 3: Mix the Wet Ingredients
1. Whisk together the Greek yogurt, olive oil, honey, and milk until smooth in another bowl.

Step 4: Make the Batter
1. Gradually add the dry ingredients to the wet ingredients, stirring until well combined.
2. Pour the batter into the prepared baking dish, smoothing the top.

Step 5: Bake the Cake
1. Bake for 30–35 minutes until the top is golden brown and a toothpick inserted in the center comes out clean.

Step 6: Prepare the Honey Syrup
1. Combine honey, water, and lemon juice in a small saucepan while the cake bakes.
2. Heat over medium-low heat, stirring until the honey dissolves.
3. Add orange blossom or rose water (if used) and simmer for 2–3 minutes. Remove from heat and set aside.

Step 7: Soak the Cake
1. Once the cake is baked, remove it from the oven and let it cool slightly.
2. Using a skewer or toothpick, poke small holes all over the surface of the cake.
3. Slowly pour the honey syrup over the cake, allowing it to soak in.

Step 8: Garnish and Serve
1. Sprinkle the top with chopped pistachios and a dusting of cinnamon (if desired).
2. Cut into small pieces and serve warm or at room temperature.

Serving Suggestions
- Serve with a dollop of Greek yogurt or a scoop of vanilla ice cream.
- Pair with a cup of mint tea or espresso for a Mediterranean-style dessert.
- Store leftovers in an airtight container at room temperature for up to 2 days.

This **Honey-Soaked Semolina Cake with Pistachios** is a delightful blend of textures and flavors, highlighting the rich culinary traditions of the Mediterranean Diet. It's perfect for any occasion. Enjoy!

7. Poached Pears in Red Wine and Spices

Yield: 2 servings | **Preparation Time:** 10 minutes | **Cooking Time:** 25–30 minutes

Ingredients	Nutritional Information (Per Serving)
For the Poached Pears • 2 medium pears (Bartlett or Anjou), peeled and stems left intact • 1 cup red wine (dry, such as Merlot or Cabernet Sauvignon) • 1/4 cup water • 2 tbsp honey or maple syrup • 1 cinnamon stick • 2 whole cloves • 1/8 tsp ground nutmeg • 1/2 tsp vanilla extract • Zest of 1/2 an orange (optional, for added citrus flavor) **Optional Customizations** • Substitute red wine with pomegranate juice for an alcohol-free option. • Add a star anise pod for a more complex flavor. • Sprinkle with chopped pistachios or almonds before serving for added texture.	• **Calories:** 180 kcal • **Protein:** 1 g • **Carbohydrates:** 34 g • **Fats:** 0 g • **Fiber:** 4 g • **Cholesterol:** 0 mg • **Sodium:** 5 mg • **Potassium:** 250 mg

Equipment Needed
- Small saucepan
- Peeler
- Slotted spoon

Step-by-Step Instructions
Step 1: Prepare the Pears
1. Peel the pears, leaving the stems intact.
2. Slice a small amount off the bottom of each pear so they can stand upright in the saucepan.

Step 2: Create the Poaching Liquid
1. In a small saucepan, combine the red wine, water, honey, cinnamon stick, cloves, nutmeg, vanilla extract, and orange zest (if using).
2. Bring the mixture to a gentle simmer over medium heat, stirring to dissolve the honey.

Step 3: Poach the Pears
1. Gently place the pears in the poaching liquid, standing upright if possible.
2. Reduce the heat to low and cover the saucepan with a lid. Simmer for 20–25 minutes, turning the pears occasionally to ensure even cooking and color.
3. The pears are done when tender and can be easily pierced with a knife.

Step 4: Reduce the Sauce
1. Using a slotted spoon, carefully remove the pears from the saucepan and set them aside.
2. Increase the heat to medium and simmer the poaching liquid until it reduces to a thick syrup (about 5–7 minutes).

Step 5: Serve
1. Place each pear on a dessert plate and drizzle with the reduced red wine sauce.
2. Garnish with a sprinkle of chopped nuts or a dollop of Greek yogurt, if desired.

Serving Suggestions
- Serve as a light dessert or a romantic dinner treat.
- Pair with a small biscotti or almond cookie for added texture.
- Enjoy warm or at room temperature.

This **Poached Pears in Red Wine and Spices** recipe is a beautiful representation of Mediterranean cuisine. It combines wholesome ingredients with an elegant presentation. This healthy and flavorful dessert is sure to impress. Enjoy!

Your free gift!

Scan the QR code to download the free
30-Day Meal Plan to Transform Your Health and Simplify Your Lifestyle.
We promise you'll love it!

Made in the USA
Las Vegas, NV
08 February 2025

17751318R00072